The North American Waterfowler

The North American

Waterfowler

by Paul S. Bernsen

WITH PAINTINGS BY LES C. KOUBA
AND PHOTOS BY BOB AND IRA SPRING

BALLANTINE BOOKS • NEW YORK

Copyright 1972 Superior Publishing Company

All rights reserved.

Library of Congress Catalog Card Number: 72-85489

This edition published by arrangement with Salisbury Press, a division of Superior Publishing Company.

SBN 345-24220-3-495

First Printing: September, 1974

Printed in the United States of America

BALLANTINE BOOKS
A Division of Random House, Inc.
201 East 50th Street, New York, N.Y. 10022
Simultaneously published by
Ballantine Books, Ltd., Toronto Canada

Dedication

This book is dedicated to our sons
and the generations yet unborn that
they will not be deprived of the legacy
to which they are entitled — Waterfowl
hunting and the sport it provides.

CONTENTS

The future of hunting lies in man's ability to maintain habitat for generations of ducks yet unborn.
Courtesy Ducks Unlimited

INTRODUCTION

The frost glistened on the cattails as the October sun peeped over the hill. His green head shone as it mirrored itself in the crystal-clear lake beneath him. Henri, the young Mallard, preened his feathers as he looked around at the Alberta lake that had been his home. He'd been born here five months earlier along with eleven brothers and sisters.

The raucous quacking all around him told him it was time to go. His father discussed some last-minute flight plans with his uncles as he dipped his bill for one last drink. The chorus of quacking picked up its pace to a deafening roar, his dad nodded and the entire surface of the lake lifted off.

The young drake crooked his neck and looked back towards his lake. In a few more days it would be ice-locked until spring. He felt the surge of power as his wing beats propelled him higher into the air currents. Beneath him stretched miles of Canadian wheat fields. He remembered dinner last night. That wheat tasted awfully good! His uncle had told him about American corn and said it was better than wheat. Soon, he'd get to try some.

Midmorning found the flock over Edmonton and the drake wondered what all those shiny contraptions were that were going in and out of the ground. He was passing over Edmonton's oil fields. The flock flew until late afternoon. Then they all followed his dad into a lake bigger than any he'd ever seen. His dad had made the trip five times and knew every lake and wheat field.

The next morning Henri had his first taste of wild rice. There was lots of competition for breakfast as several other flocks joined them. Another inquisitive drake asked him where their flock was headed. "To Washington," he replied. After breakfast the flock took off. This would be their last good meal until they crossed the U.S. border.

Several hundred miles away a man and his young son shoveled dirt around a new duck blind. They methodically backfilled the dirt until the blind's profile blended into the hill. The quiet of the October morning was broken as the man started the brush cutter. In a few moments he had cut enough sagebrush to camouflage the blind. The man and the boy carried the sagebrush over to the blind. It took an hour to wire all the sage brush over the exposed portions of the blind. A flock of honkers sailed past them and landed a couple hundred yards away. The young boy said, "Gee, Dad, I wish today was opening day."

"I know the feeling, Mike. You've only got two more days to wait." The man thought to himself how well he did know the anxiety of waiting. Since he was eight, he'd waited thrity-two times for opening day. This particular time had more significance because young Mike could shoot. They painted the inside of the blind drab olive, then called it a day.

That night the flock had only sago plant seeds for dinner. It was all that grew in this high British Columbia lake. Henri was awakened by the gabbling of the flock. A cougar stalked the shoreline, growling his disappointment over not having a Mallard for breakfast. The flock flew all day and landed early in the afternoon in the mighty Columbia River. Three miles downstream Wanapum Dam spewed power through its transmission lines.

Mike sat in the classroom fidgeting. The day had worn on slowly and he could hardly wait the thirty minutes until school was out. All day long flocks of imaginary Mallards tooled around the schoolroom and he was just about to "limit" when the teacher interrupted his shot by asking him for the paper he hadn't finished. The bell rang and he was saved from the teacher's wrath. He ran all the way home and after a scolding from his mother about his general appearance, he went to the basement and proceeded to check out his .410.

There were thousands of Mallards around Henri, waiting for what, he did not know. It was only a few moments until sunset. An incessant quacking prevailed everywhere. As the sun set, other flocks were taking off. Henri wondered where they were going at this time of night. His uncle swam over and said they would leave in a moment. Henri asked, "Where are we going?"

"To get some corn," replied his uncle.

The flock took off and flew straight east toward a place called Othello. As they flew over Highway 26, Henri noticed many more moving lights than he'd seen before. What he didn't know was that it was the evening before opening day of hunting season. Henri followed the flock until it landed next to a field of tall, wavy stuff. It had thicker stalks than salt grass and was much taller.

Mike and his dad fixed the last of the decoys. They were good decoys, each hand-painted with enough braided nylon line keeled around them to hit bottom in thirty feet of water. Mike said, "See you in the morning, Dad." Then he trotted off to bed.

Henri had stuffed himself with corn and began to wonder if he could fly. Morning came and all the flocks left the cornfield. Henri's father led the flock to a large secluded lake out in the scabrock. The water tasted good and helped wash down the corn.

Young Mike struggled with the decoy sack but was determined to do his share. His father and older brother Tony had a few steps on him and he hurried to catch up. Eleven-thirty came and the decoys were all set. The lake was like a millpond and Mike's dad hoped a breeze would pick up and give the decoys a little movement. They had been joined by an older man named Al and the four of them polished off lunch. Lots of ducks scurried back and forth as they were flushed from one lake to another. There were lots of hunters around and the birds were restless. At 11:58 two young boys had spotted Henri and the flock. They attempted to sneak the flock but were spotted and the birds flushed out of range. The boys fired anyway and Henri jumped five extra feet. "Gosh, what a noise," he thought. Henri was impressed by the shot and pulled alongside his uncle and dad.

Each lake had hunters moving around and the flock headed south a couple of miles. They spotted the decoy flock and responded to the calling. Young Mike sat nervously beside his dad as he watched the flock decoy. The other three had decided to let Mike shoot first. The flock settled toward the decoys and Mike pulled the hammer back on his .410. The closest bird was Henri and Mike pulled down on him. The afternoon sun reflected on Mike's gun and at the last second Henri flared. Mike missed and Henri flew off to join the flock. Mike was disappointed, but there will be other shots and other days, *for this is duck hunting*!

My name is Paul Bernsen. The boys are mine, Mike and Tony. The older man is Albert Salisbury, my publisher who encouraged me to write this book.

As long as there are little boys and little ducks, we have two valuable resources. The ducks will grow and so will the boys. The important thing is to help the ducks and geese grow and keep the boys interested.

This book was written with the idea of broadening the reader's knowledge not only about hunting but about conservation, sportsmanship and the value of waterfowl as a resource. This is *The North American Waterfowler*!

Chapter I
DUCKS

In this chapter we have taken the ten most sporting species of ducks and presented a short discussion of each bird. These ten ducks were chosen because they are most representative of the birds the average hunter sees. Two birds, the Canvasback and the Wood Duck, are peculiar to particular areas. They are both in trouble as to habitat and numbers. The Scaup, or Bluebill as he is sometimes called, is a familiar bird to coastal gunners and is their main target. The Mallard and Pintail, by contrast, are widely distributed and probably the best known of North American waterfowl.

These ten birds have not been presented in order of importance but according to their representation and distribution to hunters in general.

The Mallard

The Mallard or Greenhead is the best known and most highly prized duck found in North America. Its wide range and distribution make it a common target for shooters almost everywhere. This bird ranks with the Canvasback as a culinary delight. Nothing compares to a fat, grain fed Mallard to whet any hunter's appetite.

With his bright plumage the drake is easily distinguished from other ducks. In areas where both Mallards and Black Ducks are found, the hen Mallard is somtimes confused with the Black Ducks. However, both male and female Black Ducks are considerably duskier than a hen Mallard and readily distinguishable.

Adult Mallards weigh approximately three pounds at maturity. Even though it is a big bird, its speed is quite deceptive as it cruises in the forty- to sixty-mile-per-hour range. The Mallard, when surprised, has a capacity to launch itself almost straight up at a rate of climb that even a Teal would be proud of.

These ducks are good propagators and will produce seven to thirteen ducklings early in the spring. The drakes begin to color in late August or early September. They look like the hens prior to that. Both the drake and the hen develop quickly and can fly about two-and-a-half months after birth.

Most of our Mallards are raised in the Canadian Provinces and begin their southward migration in late September. Unlike the goose, a Mallard doesn't migrate by instinct but rather because of lack of food and open water. When the snowfall accumulates to the point where the Greenhead can't get at small grain such as corn, barley and wheat, he'll move out. Open water is important to him but he will grin and bear some shortage of it if there is plenty of feed. In duck hunters' lingo, migrant ducks are referred to as "Northerns." Northern Mallards usually arrive in the States the first week of November but that can vary slightly depending on weather conditions.

Mallards decoy readily and even the wiliest Mallard is a sucker for a good caller. Early in the season a half dozen decoys and a good call is quite adequate, but as the season progresses they decoy better with larger stools of decoys.

The Pintail

The Pintail or Sprig is another widely known and well-distributed duck. Because of its long neck it is easily distinguished from other ducks. In the case of the drake, his long tail feathers distinguish him better than his female counterpart. With his snow-white breast and other pronounced markings even an amateur can tell the drake from the molted brown female.

Pintails are more wary than other ducks and for that reason do not decoy as well. This duck is an excellent table bird; so much so that in California they are held in esteem over the Mallard. A bull Sprig in flight is a sight to behold. One long remembered! With their streamlined bodies, Pintails sail along easily in the fifty- to sixty-mile-per-hour class. They can however turn it on faster when under duress.

Mature Pintails are not as heavy as Mallards or Canvasbacks. The male weighs about two pounds and the female about four ounces less. In breeding they produce six to twelve ducklings. Like geese, both parents assist in raising the family.

These birds thrive on aquatic growth, i.e. seeds and grasses. Near coastal regions their diet will include shellfish. In areas where small grains are raised, they make themselves equally at home.

Unlike Mallards, as soon as the temperature drops, the Sprig heads south. He winters as far south as Panama and in the spring he will go as far north as the Northwest Territories.

With his natural wariness the larger the decoy set the better. In calling, once a Pintail files his flight plan, keep quiet. He's committed!

The Canvasback

The Canvasback, or "Can" as he has been nicknamed, has probably enjoyed more print than any of his relatives. He is a superior table bird.

This duck is a big bird and weighs in at between two and three pounds. The Canvasback is often mistaken for a male Redhead. However, if you look closely, you'll see several basic differences. In the male comparison, the drake's coloring is much more drab than the Redhead's, particularly in the region of the head. The Canvasback has a long bill while the Redhead has a shorter bill similar to a Widgeon. The former's head is sloped like a Mallard's while the latter's head is circular and abrupt. The female is easily identified from the male by its brown head and brown breast.

The Can is the fastest of all big ducks and has been timed by an airplane at seventy-five miles per hour. You can always tell when one is coming because of his pre-approach noise which sounds like a jet on descent to your decoys.

The ducklings can fly in ten weeks. Their plumage development and coloring is faster than most other ducks.

The Canvasback is the best known of the diving ducks and spends a good part of his life diving for wild celery, grasses and pond weeds. In coastal areas he eats shellfish as well as fresh and decaying fish. The ones feeding in the interior are by far the most palatable.

Canvasbacks are widely distributed and have great range and unlike most ducks are common to both the Atlantic as well as the Pacific Coast. Chesapeake Bay is an area commonly associated with the Canvasback. Their main breeding areas are located in Canada, Central Oregon and in the Minnesota lake region. Canvasbacks, like their first cousin the Redhead, have been on the decline due to drainage of nesting areas, drought and pesticide control of mosquitos. In recent years strict hunting regulations have helped to bring both species back. However, lots more work and new nesting habitat is needed for their survival.

The Canvasback is another wary duck and its exceptional speed makes it a difficult target to hit. It decoys well to large stools. In the Chesapeake Bay—Currituck Sound region two hundred decoys are not uncommon at one blind.

The Black Duck

The Black Duck is the most important duck to Atlantic Flyway gunners. His range for the most part is restricted to the Atlantic seaboard. He spends his summers in Canada, Labrador and the Great Lakes region. His winters are spent anywhere from New England to Florida. Wholesale drainage of eastern swamps for urban development has drastically reduced his range. When found, his numbers are much more concentrated.

The Black is probably the most easily identified of all birds. His vivid dusty black body and gaudy red legs make him a standout among all species of waterfowl. The biggest of North America's prime ducks, he tips the scales at slightly more than three pounds. He has many characteristics of the Mallard and is blessed with eagle-like vision. His acute sense of hearing makes him the most difficult to get by jump shooting. He usually has the jump on the hunter.

These ducks are good parents, particularly the mother who takes care of her brood in an admirable way. She usually has six to eight ducklings.

They are a lover of shellfish as well as aquatic growth. With their wariness they are extremely hard to decoy. A large stool of decoys is a must for continued success.

I have a particular fondness for Black Ducks having lived in Massachusetts until I was nineteen. I spent hundreds of hours chasing them. My mind is filled with memories. One in particular stands out. I was eleven at the time with pretty good size. My father had restricted me to shooting a single-barrel, 16-guage shotgun so as to limit the amount of shells I shot. World War II was on and shells were hard to come by. Our next door neighbor was drafted and bequeathed me his 16-gauge Browning Automatic for the duration of the war. He also gave me three boxes of shells. I told my father, "Tomorrow morning I am going to attack those Blacks." Up bright and early, I trekked to the swamp near our house and waited patiently for dawn and the first Blacks to fly out to feed. Suddenly about fifty of the most beautiful birds you ever saw came right at me, not twenty yards high. I reached up and blasted at them. Much to my amazement two came down with the first shot. I was shell-shocked! I didn't even bother to fire the other two shots. Boy, was I proud! I've shot thousands of ducks since that day in 1942 but have never equaled that thrill.

The Widgeon

The Widgeon, or Baldpate as he is sometimes called, also is pretty well-known to most scatter-gunners. The drake is easily recognized from the female by his vivid markings. His white forehead and green headpatch stand out over the other markings. The female's buff-brown head and white undercarriage put her one up in coloring over female Mallards and Pintails. Both male and female weigh approximately two pounds.

Widgeon mate in May and the youngsters greet life in early July. Hen Widgeon are super mothers and will not abandon their brood even when extreme danger presents itself.

These ducks are primarily grass-eaters. Sometimes they are thieves and get grass without diving for it. Their chief victims are Coots. When the Coot dives down and comes up with a choice morsel, the Widgeon will steal it. Lakes that have lots of Coots also have good Widgeon populations.

The Widgeon breeding grounds are extensive and range from the Corn Belt to the Bering Sea. Like his smaller cousin, the Green-winged Teal, his numbers seem to be increasing. Widgeon normally fly in the forty-mile-per-hour class but in a herky-jerky manner. There are lots of opinions on their intelligence. Having hunted them from Massachusetts to Washington, I'd say they are not one of our brighter ducks as I've had them decoy even when I was wading in the water after a deceased bird. Widgeon will decoy to any decoy including goose decoys.

The Green-winged Teal

The Green-winged Teal is noted by North American gunners for its speed, beauty and flavor. Its distribution across the U.S. and Canada makes it a favorite target for gunners. Despite its small size, three-quarters of a pound, this bird is still a heavyweight among ducks. When it comes to sporting qualities, it holds its own with any duck.

The drake is easily distinguished from any other duck in two ways: his vivid color and size. His brown head with its green striped crest and the familiar green sheathed wing feathers make him a standout among ducks. The female looks very similar to the female Blue-winged Teal except for the variance in their wing colors. A mature female is buff-brown with the undercarriage being white. They lay ten to twelve eggs each spring. The young ones can fly in ten to eleven weeks.

Teal eat mostly vegetable matter consisting of pond weeds and aquatic growth. It also likes small grains. When fish is available, usually in a dead state, Teal will fill up. Fish-fed Teal are not quite as tasty as the grain-fed variety.

The Teal is found in all of North America from the far North to Mexico. The first cold snap will hustle some of them south. The heartier birds will stick it out until freeze-up. They decoy readily and flocks of up to 100 are not uncommon when they decide to set down.

The Blue-winged Teal

The Blue-winged Teal is one of the prettiest of all waterfowl. The male's moon-like head markings make him easily distinguishable from both the Cinnamon and Green-winged Teal. The female resembles the hen Mallard in minature except for her pronounced wing markings. Both the male and female are extremely small, weighing only twelve to sixteen ounces at maturity. What it lacks in size it makes up for when it comes to flavor. Teal on toast is a favorite breakfast item at many fancy duck clubs.

Blue-wings are among the fastest of all birds, normally cruising at fifty- to sixty-miles-per-hour. They have been estimated at speeds up to a hundred ten miles per hour. Fortunately for hunters, Blue-winged Teal produce well and broods of nine to twelve are common.

These little ducks, like Mallards, are very fond of small grains. They are occasionally observed "tipping" up for food, but usually skim the surface for insects and seeds. When available they will eat shellfish which makes them less desirable than when they are on grain.

The Blue-wing is first to migrate of all ducks and migration takes him to Mexico and Central America. Summer finds the Blue-wing nesting for the most part in Northern Canadian Provinces. The Mississippi and Central Flyways get most of the shooting now. His distribution was once much broader but over-shooting and the draining of natural habitat have seriously reduced his numbers. Federal and state refuges have helped some, but more help is needed for the Blue-wing. Like all Teal he decoys well. This has also attributed to his downfall.

The Wood Duck

The male Wood Duck is the prettiest of all waterfowl and is easily identified by his multi-hued brilliant plumage. The female is not as gaudy as the male but is prettier than most female ducks. Both the male and female have short capes on their heads which is uncommon to other waterfowl.

Wood Ducks like to nest in trees and will lay nine to fourteen eggs which puts them among the more prolific waterfowl. With their liking for hollow logs and hollow tree limbs, some public-spirited hunters hit upon the idea of making some artificial nests. These nests are made out of lightweight aluminum and look very much like a one-piece mailbox with a hole in it. The nests are mounted on poles in swamps and other areas common to Wood Duck habitat. The artificial nest concept was an instant success and has been a predominate factor in his ability to survive.

With its willingness to decoy and its high desirability by hat makers and fly tiers, its numbers were so drastically reduced that it was necessary to set bag limits and restrict its seasons. Most states still allow only one Wood Duck to be taken.

The Wood Duck flies like a Woodcock, in a weavy, twisting manner through his wooded habitat. His speed is fast and graceful in the thirty-five- to forty-five-mile-per-hour range. Wood Ducks feed on acorns and beechnuts as well as chestnuts and pecans when available. They also eat insects and various aquatic plants — swamp peas being a favorite.

His eastern range is confined mainly to the Atlantic Coast and west to the Mississippi River Valley then north to Southern Canada. His western range extends north into British Columbia and south through Washington, Oregon, California and Mexico. An easy bird to decoy, it is a very popular bird particularly with eastern gunners.

The Greater Scaup

The Greater Scaup or Bluebill is primarily a coastal bird found principally on the Atlantic and Pacific Coasts as well as the Great Lake region. Because of its high shellfish consumption, it doesn't have the table appeal of some of the other birds. Scaup are hardy birds and can stand extremely cold temperatures. An expert diver and swimmer, its large feet assist in taking it to depths some of the other ducks wouldn't tackle.

Both the male and female weigh about two pounds. The male being typical of most ducks is extremely handsome with a black breast and a white undercarriage and green back. His short neck supports a green head and the famous blue bill. The female has a brown breast, white undercarriage, and her back is brown-grey. Her brown head is highlighted by a parrot-like white patch located just above her blue bill.

Scaup have six to ten offspring each year. Their diet is for the most part shellfish, particularly oysters and mussels. They do however eat pond weeds and other aquatic plants when available.

Scaup winter on both the Atlantic and Pacific Coasts. Their nesting areas are among the most extreme of all waterfowl as they nest as far north as the Arctic with Northern Canada and Alaska supporting most of them. Scaup are an easy bird to decoy. However, for the most part, you'll need extremely long decoy lines because of the depth of the water the birds frequent.

The Gadwall

The Gadwall along with some of his cousins are decreasing in number. Drought and draining of marsh-lands for agricultural purposes are the chief contributing factors. In recent years botulism has bothered this species particularly in the west. He is still, however, an important sporting duck especially on the West Coast.

The Gadwall would be classified as a medium-sized duck, weighing about two pounds at maturity. The drake differs from the female by his composite grey cast. The female is spotted brown. Both have white blended into their secondary wing feathers. The Gadwall is not as swift as the other big ducks but can still make thirty-five to forty-five-miles per-hour.

A good producer, the female Gadwall will raise as many as thirteen young ones. Gadwall are principally vegetarians, eating aquatic plants and weed seeds. They will however eat minnows and small fish when available. In the west it frequently flies into grain fields to feed right along with the Mallard.

The Gadwall is one of the few cross flyway birds. In leaving their nesting areas of the Western Canadian Provinces they will fly a southeasterly route to reach the Atlantic Flyway for the winter. The Gadwall is one of the easiest of all ducks to decoy and responds readily to any good stool.

Pacific Flyway

Chapter 2
BLINDS

There are three ingredients that make for successful duck hunting: good blinds, good decoys and good calling. I consider good blinds the most important item. You can have poor decoys or no decoys at all and still get birds if the blinds are good and are located in the right place. While calling ducks is important it isn't necessarily the determining factor in the amount of birds you'll get. If your blind is located in an area the birds are using you'll still get your share. Forget your call some morning and you'll see what I mean. Blinds take lots of work but the work will produce birds. Your results will be proportional to the effort expended.

Before installing blinds, the area should be thoroughly studied. Get out early several mornings and watch the birds. Study their habits. See what effect the wind has on them. Then and only then build your blinds and build them well. A blind is your home away from home. When you build it keep in mind you'll be spending many hours in it. A blind should be comfortable, dry and still offer enough room to move around in so that you're not restricted when it comes time to shoot.

We have pictured several blinds in this chapter, some of which are made out of natural materials, some not. We believe there is a blind for every condition, as well as some that can be adapted to meet the unusual. Each blind is discussed in depth.

Permanent Blinds

There are two considerations in the installation of permanent blinds. The first is the length of time you have control of the property. If you own the property or have a long-term lease, you can without question justify the expenditure for permanent blinds. The second consideration is cost. If you don't own the property and have a short lease then it's hard to justify spending much money on blinds. This doesn't rule out putting in permanent blinds, it simply calls for some modification. If the term of your lease is of short duration or you're trying to conserve money, then we would install a blind that was not permanent, yet movable. This is not as complex as it might sound. Permanent blinds can be made of two materials: wood or some form of rock. Rock is obviously not movable, but wood is. So when you have a short lease or you are concerned about cost use a wood blind.

Installed uncamouflaged Piano Blind.

The Piano Blind

The blind that has the greatest amount of adaptability is the Piano Blind. It can be used in multitudes of situations, is low in cost and simple to install.

The Piano blind gets its name from its shape as the only music that emits from it is the melodic bang-bang from your shotgun. The Piano blind is lightweight and easily moved. We make ours in five sections: front, back, two sides and the roof. The roof consists of a single piece of 1/4-inch plywood. The other sections are made of two-by-fours and 3/4-inch plywood. The blind has a built-in backrest and a movable seat. It can be assembled in ten minutes. We use double-headed eight-penny nails. If you feel like moving, simply pull the nails. By using double-headed nails you won't fracture the wood upon removing the nails.

The roof is secured with galvanized four-penny roofing nails. The door can be installed either on the right or left side. The terrain involved will determine that. The door is hinged and has a simple hooking device.

Dry, warm and comfortable, it will accommodate two hunters and a dog. Because of this blind's popularity we have printed the actual blueprint as the end sheets of the book.

The Natural Rock Blind

The Natural Rock blind as mentioned before is an excellent permanent blind. It must however be utilized under the right conditions. In Chapter 3, Blind Locations, we show how to determine which blind is best for each situation.

This blind is of simple construction and using native rock it is low in cost. The approximate overall length is 7 feet, height is 4 feet and the depth

Fabricated Rock Blind installed in natural conditions.

would vary from 4 to 5 feet. The reason we hedge on the actual dimensions is due to the variance in rock sizes. It is impossible to get absolute conformity in each blind.

When you've selected the right site and assured yourself there is enough rock for the job, site preparation begins. The surface area of the blind should be leveled to insure a solid foundation. If some obstructions stick up, they can be flattened with a sledgehammer or crowbar.

You'll need these additional items: shovel, wire, hoe, premix cement, cement trowels, stone hammer, wire cutters, a level and a tub to mix the cement in. Lightweight cotton gloves should be worn to protect your hands in using the cement. Continued emersing in cement will cause your hands to crack and bleed. In the illustration you'll notice wire hoops sticking out from some of the joints. Their purpose is to hold the camouflage. Light wire of about sixteen gauge is fine for the hoops. In a blind of this size, if you don't go too heavy on the cement, ten sacks is adequate.

Great care must be used in mixing the cement. Don't get it too sloppy. The cement should have just enough consistency for easy handling. Don't mix too much in advance as it will dry out.

The rocks you use should be reasonably uniform. In building this arced wall, select rocks that are as flat on the bottom and the top as possible. When you lay a tier you can level up with extra cement. As each tier is laid, insert several wire hoops in the joints while the cement is still wet. When camouflage is placed in the hoops it will give you 6 inches to 8 inches more cover in front.

In building a wall of 4 feet it will normally take about six tiers of rock. After you have achieved your desired height, put a 2 inch cap on the top. This will serve to mold the wall together. If it's exceptionally hot take the used cement sacks, soak them and place them on the cap. This will shade the wall and protect the cement from drying out too fast. Let the cement cure for a few days before installing the suspended roof which is shown here.

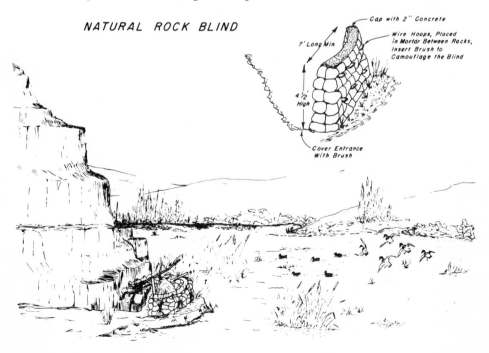

NATURAL ROCK BLIND

Cap with 2" Concrete

Wire Hoops, Placed in Mortar Between Rocks, Insert Brush to Camouflage the Blind

7' Long Min

4 1/2 High

Cover Entrance With Brush

The Suspended Roof

The Suspended Roof is a necessity for both the Natural Rock blind as well as our next blind, the Block blind. Usually both blinds are put on points that have banks behind them. The bank is dug out in such a manner as to allow the roof to be suspended over the blind below. The opening should be reduced to about 22 inches which is ample room for shooting. Each roof has to be adjusted to the particular terrain involved.

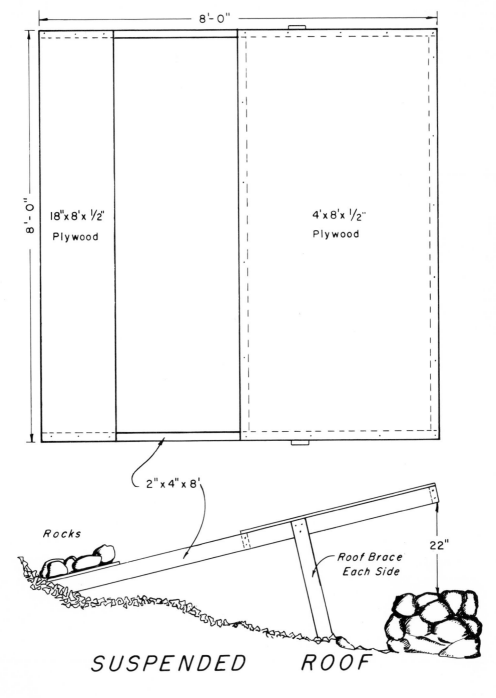

8'- 0"

8'- 0"

18"x 8'x ½"
Plywood

4'x 8'x ½"
Plywood

2"x 4"x 8'

Rocks

Roof Brace
Each Side

22"

SUSPENDED   ROOF

The suspended roof is simple in its design. We use an 8-by-4-foot sheet of 1/2-inch *exterior* plywood. The plywood is nailed to a border of two-by-fours. The 8-foot-by-18-inch piece of plywood which holds the rocks is also nailed to the two-by-fours. Both the plywood and the two-by-fours should be painted with olive duckboat paint. Besides helping camouflage, the paint will also preserve the wood.

Suspension is accomplished by placing rocks on the 8-foot-by=18-inch piece of plywood. Then dig a small hole on each side of the roof for the two-by-fours braces. The braces should be long enough to allow the roof to be lifted up at such an angle to allow enough headroom for the shooters as they rise to shoot. The braces should then be nailed to the roof.

The Block Blinds

When you have an area under long-term control, Block Blinds are suggested. If the area is void of usable natural rock or you feel you'd rather work with block, you have two choices of block material: pumice block and circular cesspool block. If you have no aversion to square blinds, pumice block is very desirable. Light in weight, you can lay them as fast as you can mortar the joints and level them.

If the contour of the terrain calls for a tapered blind, then the circular block used in cesspool construction is best. It is a little harder to handle because of its heavier weight.

As we discussed in constructing Natural Rock Blinds, site preparation is important. The ground should be as nearly level as possible. You'll need all the items used on Natural Rock Blinds as well as a stone chisel to break blocks in the finishing of a tier. The wire hoops are placed in the wet joints as the tiers are completed. Unlike Natural Rock Blinds it may be necessary

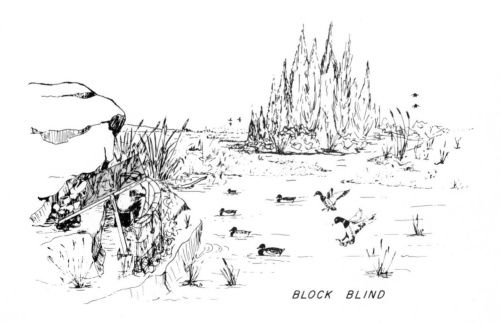

BLOCK BLIND

24

to paint the exposed portions of the block. Again, olive duckboat paint does a good job. The suspended roof is installed in the same manner as outlined in the construction of the Natural Rock Blind.

The Pillbox Blind

The Pillbox Blind is a modification of the Piano Blind. It is completely square in shape and has a small suspended roof. Eighty percent of the blind is below ground. Its usage is restricted mainly to moderately flat areas adjacent to water where the terrain makes it unadvisable to have a large profile above ground. The blind must be installed in dry ground, high enough so that water cannot enter the blind. The blind is comprised of four panels each 5 feet high and 5 feet wide. As in the case of the Piano Blind they can be assembled in ten minutes and again we use sixteen-penny double-headed nails. One panel has a backrest and becomes the rear panel. Two of the others each have a two-by-four cross brace which supports the seat. As most

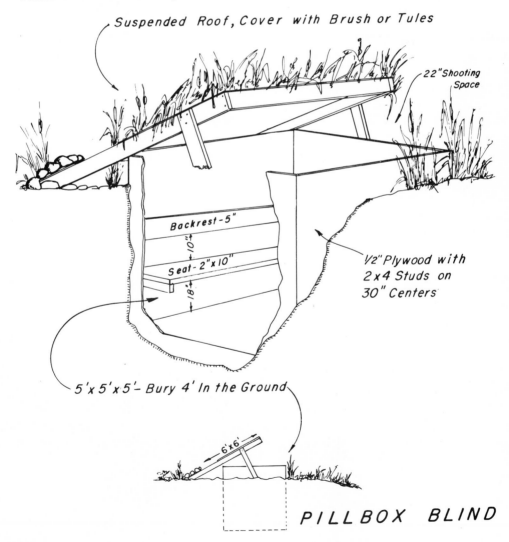

Suspended Roof, Cover with Brush or Tules

22" Shooting Space

Backrest - 5"

Seat - 2" x 10"

½" Plywood with 2 x 4 Studs on 30" Centers

5' x 5' x 5' - Bury 4' In the Ground

6' x 6'

PILLBOX BLIND

of the blind is normally covered by earth, it reduces camouflage to a minimum. The suspended roof is cut down to a piece of 3/4-inch plywood, 5-feet square and is nailed to two 6-foot-two-by-four runners. We again use two-by-four angled roof supports nailed just high enough to insure head room. A one foot wide piece of 3/4-inch plywood, 5 feet long will support the rocks necessary to help support the roof. Exposed wood surfaces should be painted and you'll need a strong box to get in and out of the blind. If you have youngsters shooting they can use the box to stand on; make sure it is good and sturdy.

Tank Blinds

Tank Blinds are also permanent blinds. The shooting potential has to be super to justify their installation. But if they are properly located they'll produce birds not only for shooters using them, but also the people in the other blinds. With a Tank Blind you have excellent bird control because it restricts the birds from leaving the lake or pothole as rapidly as they normally do. A Tank Blind is referred to as a Cutoff blind. In Chapter 3 we illustrate where they should be located.

Tank Blinds are only practical in shallow bodies of water, or in areas that can be flooded, as they must be installed when the water area is dry. Tank Blinds cost about $400 built and installed, but are worth their weight in ducks under the right conditions. The blinds are made from sheets of steel welded together to form a tank 6 feet long, 5 feet high and 4½ feet wide. The back of the tank forms a backrest and the seat supports are welded in.

The steel top rolls back on file cabinet-type roller carriage guides. Hooks are welded around the top. These are used to hold the camouflage cloth which covers the top and exposed sides and ends. A steel strip is welded on each end. A hole is drilled through which the cable passes. The cable is fixed to a steel plate or some heavy item such as a car door. Then dump about a ton of rocks on each steel plate. This holds the tank from moving. Then fill around the excavation in which the tank sits.

The weight of the dirt, rocks and steel plate prevent the tank from floating which it would do as soon as the area filled with water. The entire tank should be painted prior to installation with no-sheen black paint, both as an anti-rusting measure and for camouflage purposes. They should be bailed out and allowed to dry out any time they have been underwater. A few days before hunting season opens cut several willow shoots and place them around the blind. They'll break up the outline and will stay green for several weeks.

Any sheet metal or steel fabricating shop can build one in a day. Many years ago I helped install my first one which has since produced over a hundred geese and several hundred ducks.

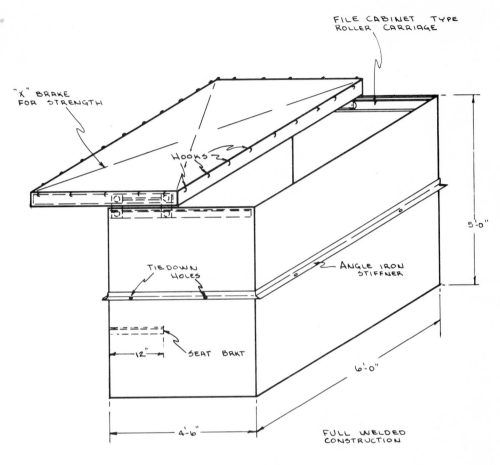

FILE CABINET TYPE
ROLLER CARRIAGE

"X" BRAKE
FOR STRENGTH

HOOKS

TIEDOWN
HOLES

ANGLE IRON
STIFFNER

5'-0"

12"

SEAT BRKT

6'-0"

4'-6"

FULL WELDED
CONSTRUCTION

Tank Blind

Temporary Blinds

Temporary blinds are blinds that you'd use if you had some doubts about how long you'd have the use of the property, or you had a question about a particular spot. Rather than pile up brush, rocks, etc., I still prefer the comfort of a good blind. In a situation that called for a temporary blind I'd use our previously illustrated Piano blind. Easily moved, I wouldn't even dig it down. Camouflage it well with natural materials and use it. If it works leave it permanently. I frequently do this when I'm trying out an area. If you don't want to go to the trouble of hauling a blind around you can stand in the tules, sit in the brush or hide in whatever cover is available. Throw out a few decoys and you're in business.

Floating Blinds

The main function of the Floating Blind is to enable the hunter to get out with the birds. In deep water it's about the only type of blind that will work. The trick in using it is to anchor it where large rafts of birds consistently stay. It should be installed much in advance of the hunting season so that the birds are used to it.

The ideal places to locate them are large lakes, coastal bays, tidal flats and swamps. Because they float, water fluctuations have no effect on them. It is important to have them securely anchored. This is accomplished by running a rope through the anchor hook and tying it to a heavy object which you then lower to the bottom. The blind should be anchored down on two opposite sides. This gives the blind good stability. Car doors available at any wrecking yard make good anchors.

In camouflaging this blind it should be made to look like a small island. In an area that has lots of brush along its shoreline you should use that particular type brush. If cattails and salt grass abound, you should use them.

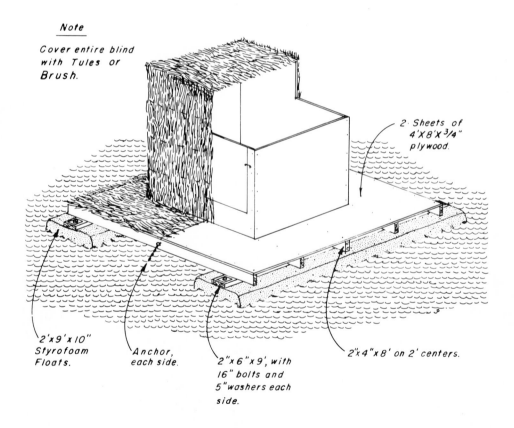

Note

Cover entire blind with Tules or Brush.

2 Sheets of 4'X8'X ³/4" plywood.

2'x9'x10" Styrofoam Floats.

Anchor, each side.

2"x6"x9', with 16" bolts and 5"washers each side.

2"x4"x8' on 2' centers.

FLOATING BLIND

All camouflage can be wired on. In coastal areas where no natural camouflage is available, the blind and platform should be painted with duckboat paint and covered with camouflage netting — the type used in World War II.

Floating Blinds should be camouflaged on shore and then towed to where they're going to be used. After the season they should be beached on dry land. This reduces wear and tear on them. You'll need transportation to the blinds and someone operating on shore who can also pick up your dead birds.

Our Floating Blind consists of a Piano Blind secured to a floating platform. The platform gets its flotation from the hugh pieces of styrofoam which are bolted to the platform. The exact dimensions are shown here in our illustration. The blind will hold two shooters and a dog comfortably. The cost of the blind is about $150 including materials and labor.

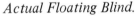
Actual Floating Blind.

Portable Blinds

We use Portable blinds under a variety of conditions. If you are trying out a spot on your property they are quite practical. Sometimes a heavy wind will force the birds into a sheltered bay they might not normally use. It is nice to be able to pick up and move to where the birds are. Portable blinds are great for public hunting areas where it's impractical to build a blind.

You can make the best Portable blind in the world in an hour. All you need is some camouflage netting and ten 4½-foot one-by-twos sharpened at the base. Paint these stakes with duckboat paint, both sides. Cut a piece of camouflage netting 15 feet long and 4 feet wide. Staple the netting on each stake 6 inches above the sharpened point. The stakes should be placed in 18-inch intervals.

When you get to the spot you're going to hunt, drive the stakes into the ground forming a circle. The size of the circle can be varied according to your needs. When not in use, roll the blind up, tie it and it is ready to be used again.

Camouflage netting has been in use by the military since World War II. You can usually obtain it when available by calling the salvage officer at the nearest army base. I recently obtained some at Fort Lewis, Washington. It is sold by the bale. My cost was $1.00 per bale and each bale will make three to four portable blinds.

10 - 1" x 2" x 4'-6"
Stakes

Drive into
Mudline

PORTABLE BLIND

Pits

Pits have many uses, both for ducks as well as geese. Both birds frequent the same area and where possible the pits should be designed toward that end. In Chapter 3, we deal with the specific locations.

A Pit is merely a hole in the ground. It's there for one reason, to hide the hunter. It is used because the terrain won't permit a blind to be constructed above ground.

There are three methods of creating a Pit:

1. Digging it by hand
2. Using a backhoe
3. Using Dynamite

Years ago I used to dig by hand twenty or thirty Pits. I then graduated to hiring a backhoe and this got pretty expensive. I finally got smart and started using dynamite. Dynamite is the cheapest work force you can employ and also the most efficient. Properly used it makes a nice clean Pit. In Chapter 4, we discuss its use in construction of blinds.

The Pit should be large enough to accommodate two shooters. Five feet long, 3 feet wide and 4 feet deep are normally considered pretty good dimensions. Its sides should be shaved smooth to eliminate dirt from falling inside. If caving in is a problem you may have to shore up the sides with plywood, or make a frame. A Pit obviously makes a large opening which the birds can look into. You can reduce this opening either by placing tree limbs or brush over the ends and along the sides. This still gives enough shooting room. In the case of stubble fields or cornfields an old screen door will do

RIVER PIT

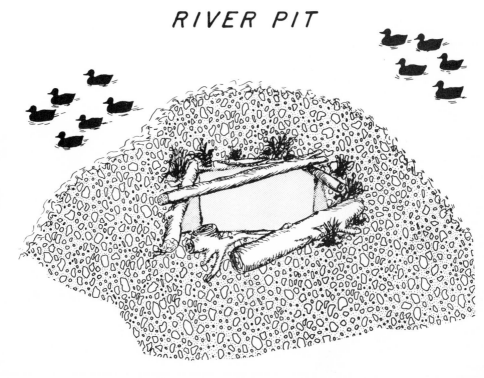

Blind is located on pronounced spit in river.

31

the job. The door is placed over the rear portion of the Pit. When birds are coming the door is pulled forward; as soon as the birds are in range push the door back. The ground behind the door should be smooth so that the door is easily movable.

Commercial Blinds

If you don't feel like getting involved in the labor of building blinds there is a shortcut — a Commercial blind. Normally I wouldn't consider a Commercial blind as being too practical but there is one now available that has some ready adaptability to quite a few places and situations. It's manufactured in Richmond, California by its inventor Henry Smith.

Made of fiber glass, the blind is watertight and colored to blend with marshy areas. Installed, it's easily anchored in place and provides maximum comfort for one shooter.

The blind has several unique and extraordinary features. A special seat rotates 360°, giving the shooter maximum mobility; yet it turns in a manner which always gives the user a backrest. The lid provides protection from the weather as well as concealment and still permits a full view of the horizon. The lid raises and swivels so as to not restrict the shooter's mobility.

When you stand up to shoot you're automatically positioned in the center of the opening. Because the bulk of the blind is below ground there is almost no profile showing. This is important for successful shooting. As you can see from the cutaway view shown here, the blind provides dry storage for shells, clothing, food, etc. The cost of the blind is $395 FOB the factory. You may obtain the blind by writing: Smitty's Duck Blinds, P.O. Box 611, Station A, Richmond, California 94808.

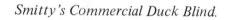

Cutaway View — Smitty's Duck Blind.   *Smitty's Commercial Duck Blind.*

 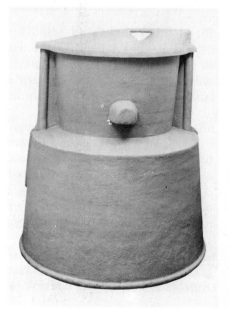

Chapter 3
BLIND LOCATIONS

We can build the best blinds in the world but they won't do much good if they're installed in the wrong place. Several factors go into what constitutes the right place.

1. Bird Traffic. How many birds pass over the area?
2. Are the birds feeding there or resting there?
3. Shelter. Do the birds use the area all the time or just when it's windy or freezing conditions exist?
4. Accessibility to the blinds?

In commenting on the four points just mentioned, the most important things are observation and common sense. You have to analyze in each situation what attracts the birds to the area or what forces them to use it.

Bird Traffic

In point No. 1, Bird Traffic, it boils down to bird usage which you can determine by observation which should be done mornings and evenings in order to be accurate. Look for pronounced points of land the birds pass over regularly, or ridges they fly over in flying in and out of the lake. Little islands in lakes are great particularly if part of the shoreline is flat so that they can swim up to shore and rest.

Feeding or Resting Birds

In point No. 2, as to whether the birds are feeding there or resting, it is again a case of observation. Puddle ducks feed in very shallow water. Therefore, the blind should be adjacent to reasonably shallow water if the birds are using it for feeding. Conversely, most diving ducks find their food in deeper water along cliffs, bays, and in salt water. Blinds should be located on spits the birds pass over or peninsulas the birds fly across in going from one body of water to another. If the diving birds are rafted in deep water and there is no adjacent land, then floating blinds are the only solution.

If the birds are merely resting on the body of water, then the blinds should be installed on spits, peninsulas, bays or islands. Floating blinds and the use of scull boats are also quite effective. The important thing is to watch the birds. If a flock of birds use a given spot, another flock will also. Try in your mind to determine the conditions that cause the birds to use the area. From these observations you can find other places for blind installations.

Shelter

In point No. 3, Shelter, we now must consider that the birds will use these areas only part of the time. They only use these areas because of climatic conditions, either wind or freezing temperatures. In the case of wind, ducks like sheltered bays, potholes and streams that get them out of the wind. In the case of bays, the blind should be located so that it faces calm water. An example of this would be, in a wind blowing from the north, a bay that had a high north bank would be sheltered; conversely the same bay in a south wind would afford the birds no protection at all.

As to potholes and streams, potholes usually lie in depressions and have one or more sides sheltered. This becomes a case of determining the most prevalent wind direction. The blind should be installed on the side that is sheltered from the wind the greatest percentage of the time.

Streams have enough natural cover that they always offer a certain amount of protection from the wind. In addition, they normally don't freeze and will offer shooting when everything else is frozen. Blinds should be located on pronounced "bends" in the stream and also on points of land in the stream that birds fly over. Ducks, in flying up or down stream, will always fly across a piece of land rather than follow the arc of the stream.

When freezing conditions exist, duck hunting becomes a whole new ball game because areas that were open when temperatures were up are now frozen. This forces the birds to use areas they might not normally use. Streams, springs and larger lakes are good when things freeze-up.

One of your more profitable days can be spent looking your entire area over to see what isn't frozen during your coldest cycle. By area, I mean, within a twenty-mile radius of where you live. Even if you find a lake that has only a small spot open, birds will get a drink, then sit on the ice. Follow them to the fields they're using and this will produce shooting. Pit blinds or a pile of cornstalks or tumbleweeds will be adequate for good field shooting.

Accessibility

When you're building blinds you have to take into account how accessible they are. Cliff blinds, for example, are fine for younger hunters; but getting to them might work a real hardship on an older person. I personally have never spared the horses in putting blinds in difficult places because they are as a rule usually highly productive. But you should consider that they might not be very easy for someone else. Try to install devices such as ladders, rope guides, etc. This will make it easier on older people or people with physical impairments.

When you install a floating blind, you also have to realize that the people shooting out of them will have to be delivered to them and picked up when the shooting is over.

In shooting swamps, it's a good idea to drive in a couple stakes and tie a rope between them running from the blind to shore. This should be done after you've picked a good route.

Most of the things we discussed regarding accessibility are common sense items; but they have to be considered.

Synopsis of Blind Locations

Lakes
1. Points of land
2. Peninsulas
3. Sheltered bays
4. Cliffs
5. Islands
6. Springs
7. Floating blinds

Streams
1. Spits of land
2. Fast water for freeze-up shooting
3. Entrances to lakes

Fields
1. For geese stick to high ridges where they're feeding. Geese will always pick the highest spots so they can have a good vantage point while they're feeding.
2. For ducks it depends on what they're feeding in. In corn use piled up cornstalks or tumbleweeds. In wheat, barley and pea fields, pits are best. But blinds built in irrigation ditches and fence rows out of tumbleweeds work fine.

Salt Water
1. Points of land
2. Cliffs
3. Islands
4. Floating blinds

Swamps
1. Adjacent to largest patch of open water for decoying purposes.
2. Along any flowing water passing through swamp.
3. Where birds consistently feed.

Potholes
1. Most sheltered part of pothole.
2. In shallow ends where birds feed.
3. At cutoff points. If one end of pothole is open and the other three sides are enclosed (high banks), the blind should be installed at the open end. This prohibits the birds from flying out without being shot at. With a blind at the opposite end you have complete bird control.

In order to better illustrate the various locations pertaining to blind locations, some aerial photos have been "shot" of typical lakes and potholes.

The aerials were "shot" to a scale of one inch equals 1,000 feet so that although the blinds might appear somewhat clustered that's not the case.

In each aerial the arrows point in exactly the direction the blinds should be faced. The photos are all printed so that north is the top of the page and south is the bottom. The left-hand margin is west and the right hand margin is east. In the aerial photos, some portions of the photos appear slightly darker than the rest of the picture. This is particularly true in the vicinity of the blinds. In most instances the darker areas represent cliffs. Each arrow indicates an actual blind we have installed and each blind is still in operation. We'll take each aerial and explain why the blinds are located where they are.

Aerial I

In Aerial 1, we find six installed blinds. It was never my intention that all six blinds be "shot" at the same time. The six blinds give us some flexibility under different conditions. The two blinds together on the east side are located at the base of a cliff. The wind here blows from the east a good percentage of the time. The birds have a natural inclination to seek the protection offered by the cliffs. The little pothole on the left side of the photo is good for the same reason — shelter from an east wind. The blind is located where it is because it's the best vantage point. It's also high and dry.

The blind slightly north of it is at the entrance to a small shallow bay where the birds like to feed and rest. The blind on the north end of the peninsula serves two purposes: It's close enough to the water to run a decoy operation and it also provides good pass shooting as most of the birds passing from the main part of the lake fly right over the blind. The most northerly blind is located on a good spit and is also at the entrance of another lake. It gets good "bird traffic."

All of these blinds were dynamited out of solid rock. The blind on the peninsula took four days to install, but it was worth it. There is considerable virtue to aerial photos as they give you a "duck's-eye" view of the operation. There is sometimes trial and error in blind installations and we had at least two other blinds installed on this lake. They were both removed for lack of activity.

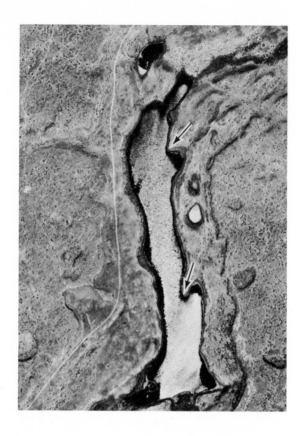

Aerial 2

A relatively short lake and a simple one to diagnose. The two pronounced spits each have small sheltered bays to the south of them. These blinds shoot fine in an east or north wind; poorly in a south or west wind. From the most northerly blind you can keep an eye on the little pothole at the north end and after a few birds accumulate in it, you can go jump it.

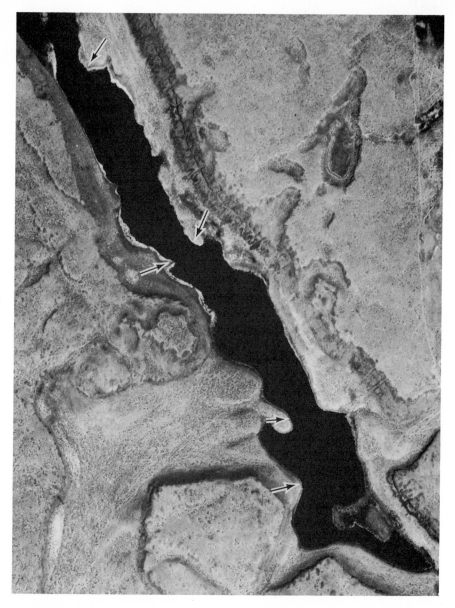

Aerial 3

An extremely long lake, almost one-and-a-half miles. We installed five blinds on it. All of the blinds are located on points of land. The two blinds to the south are separated by a small quiet bay and will shoot 90 percent of the time.

The blinds in the middle kind of block the "Khyber Pass" as the lake becomes very narrow at that point. We do, however, only shoot one blind at a time depending on which way the wind is blowing. If it's blowing from the east, we shoot the east blind; if it's blowing from the west, we shoot the west blind. As you can see from the dark areas in the photo, the lake is surrounded by high cliffs and offers quite a bit of protection for the birds. This lake has been extremely productive and will average 750 birds a year.

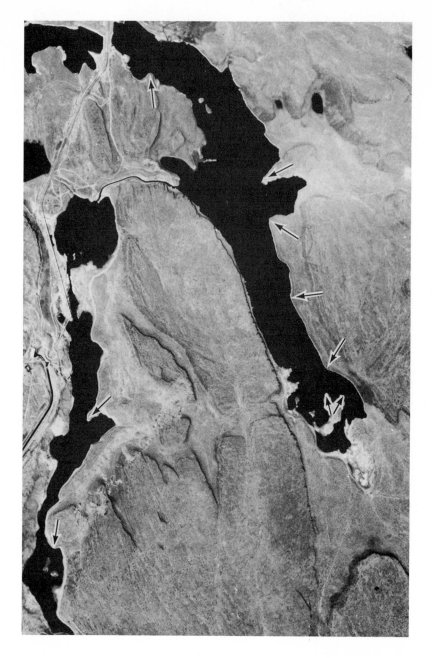

Aerial 4

Another long lake over one-and-a-half miles. You'll note most of the blinds are on the east side of the lake. The birds prefer the east side because of its high cliffs and resulting shelter. The most northerly blind covers a small bay as well as being on a nice spit. The two upper blinds on the east side cover the entrance to the large bay. When the wind blows from the north, thousands of birds raft up in the bay. Those blinds produce just as well when it is calm because of their location on the spits.

Continuing down the lake, the next two blinds on the lake offer unique shooting. They are 40 to 50 feet above the water and as a result you're shooting down on the birds a good percentage of the time. This calls for some tricky calculations on some of the shots. The two blinds farthest south on the island shoot best in a north wind as the birds all swing by them into the bay. An extremely deep lake, it takes 90 feet of decoy line to hit bottom. In big lakes like these you need large stools of decoys, at least 50 to a set.

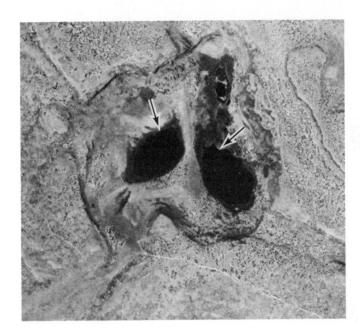

Aerial 5

In this scene we deal with small potholes. Installing blinds on small potholes can be tricky at best. The birds will pick a particular spot and will invariably all use the same place. The shelter angle is minimal here because basically all potholes offer some degree of shelter anyway.

It's been our experience that if there's a swampy end the birds will use it. They like to get out and waddle and rest. The shallow ends also produce a little food that Mr. Duck can nibble on if he's hungry.

In the two potholes pictured here, the darker cast represents swamp. Care must be exercised not to get the blinds too close to the water. Because of the high profiles of the other blinds, pillbox-type blinds are the blinds best suited for this type situation. Potholes like these should be shot only once a week.

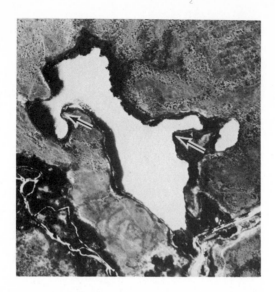

Aerial 6

In Aerial 6, we have a small lake. It has two small peninsulas extending into it. On each side of the blinds there is a sheltered bay. In a lake like this, it's not necessary to have a large stool of decoys, because birds interested in coming in will decoy just as well to 6 or 8 decoys as they will to two dozen.

Aerial 7

Again we have a long lake but we haven't put too many blinds on it. The blind to the north sticks out pretty well in the lake and every bird going up and down the lake will see the stool of decoys. In the case of the double blinds, we put two blinds in because the bay they guard is fantastic; you rarely see such a pronounced spit next to a nice bay like this. If you only installed one blind somebody would always feel deprived.

Although you can only see 4 blinds, there are actually 5. The most southerly blind has another blind in front of it but it's under water. This particular lake is subject to rather severe water fluctuations. The lower blind shoots when the water is down and the one shown in the picture shoots when the water is up. The water fluctuation is attributed to the irrigation canal at the left. Water is periodically discharged into the lake causing 15-to-20-foot variances. The problem is overcome with high-water and low-water blinds. The good bay shown here justifies the effort.

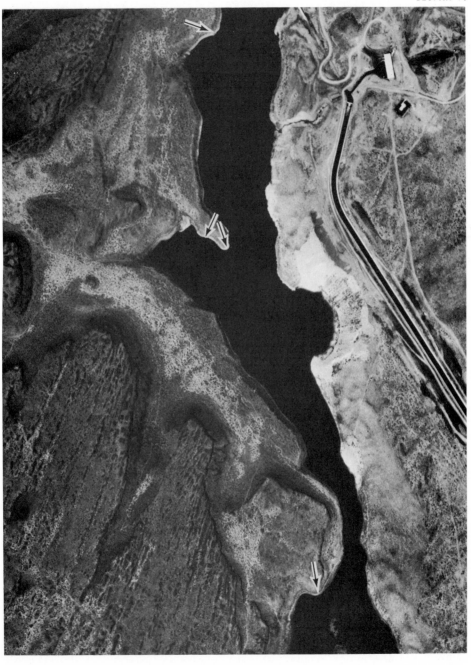

Chapter 4
BLIND CONSTRUCTION, INSTALLATION AND CAMOUFLAGE

Blind Construction — Wood

Blind construction will never be very easy and it's easier when organized. If you're going to build very many blinds then you had better plan your work and work your plan. Anything over 4 blinds calls for an assembly line. In the case of wood blinds, they should be cut like "kits." Cut all of the studs at the same time. Seats, backrests and braces can all be cut at once. The plywood for backs, sides and roof can all be cut to size producing efficiency and minimizing waste.

Assembly

The panels to all the blinds should be assembled somewhere other than the installation site. Nothing is worse than trying to do some "wood butchering" on location. Assembled blind panels can easily be hauled by vehicle to the blind site. If the terrain prohibits their being hauled, then lash them together and tow them by boat.

Blind Construction — Rock

If the blinds are to be constructed out of natural rock or block, then you must get enough rock or sufficient block to the site to complete the job. If the site lacks enough natural rock, you can haul it by boat or vehicle. Blocks can also be hauled. As we mentioned in Chapter 2, pumice block is the easiest to handle because of its lightness.

How to Cut Costs

If you anticipate building many blinds you should buy in bulk. Single-unit purchases will never save money. If you were to buy fifty sheets of plywood, for example, you'd save at least a dollar a sheet by buying them in quantity. In the case of plywood, always specify "exterior grade." It's not only cheaper but lasts longer.

Two-by-fours, nails, hinges and concrete blocks can all be bought cheaper in quantity. The ideal situation, of course, is to have a contractor or lumber dealer in your club.

Blind Installation

Once you've selected the site, the next step is to prepare the site for the blind installation. The most important consideration here is to make the blind blend into the surroundings. This is accomplished by reducing the profile of the blind. In order to reduce the profile it is necessary, at least temporarily, to remove an area of ground large enough to accommodate a blind.

The reason I use the term "at least temporarily" regarding the removal of the earth and rock at the blind site is because earth removed from the blind site should be restored exactly as it was prior to its removal. By backfilling the dirt around the blind you reduce the amount of camouflage required to cover the exposed portions of the blind.

There are two methods of removing the earth and rock from the blind site. The first method is hand removal — shovels, picks, crowbars, etc. If the digging is good this is fine, but if you have basalt outcroppings or lava formations you have problems. If the terrain precludes hand digging, method number two is used — *dynamite*! *Dynamite* is like using Mr. Clean. The dirt and rock disappear and the excavated blind site remains. Never pass up a blind site because of the terrain. If the birds are using that area, then the blind should be installed there! Your willingness to work a little harder to get more birds is often the difference between successful and unsuccessful shooting.

The Use of Dynamite in Blind Installations

The use of dynamite *anytime* is *dynamite*! Those little sticks are among the most lethal forces on earth. In the hands of amateurs, there can be trouble. If someone involved in the site preparation is not skilled and knowledgeable in the fine art of dynamiting, I suggest you hire the services of a professional powder monkey. A powderman usually gets $200 per day depending on the conditions. However, you can occasionally find somebody who "blasts" for a construction company who is willing to do a little "moonlighting." You can have a little work party and with shovels and bars, you can dig a hole down deep enough to permit him to "shoot" the site.

If the underlying rock strata precludes getting the "shooting" hole down far enough, generally eighteen inches, then resort to more drastic methods. At this point lease a portable jackhammer and gas-operated compressor. Rental will run about $25 a day. As these rigs are generally on trailers, you can haul them almost anywhere via four-wheel-drive rigs. Compressors normally have at least 100 feet of hose so this gives you a little more flexibility. With the aid of the jackhammer, you can drill "charge holes" in solid rock. If you get all the "charge holes" ready, the powder man can easily shoot 10 blind sites per day.

When a powderman knows his work, it's simple to clean out the site, level it and install the blind. If the blasted rock can be mortared, it might be a natural site for a stone blind. If the rock is too fractured then a prefab Piano Blind is the next best solution.

Advice on the Use of Dynamite

Dynamite itself is now hard to come by! With all the militants running around, many states have imposed rather stringent laws pertaining to its use. The State of Washington, where I live, is no exception. I have both a Purchaser's License and a Blaster's License but still have to account for every stick.

If you wish to gain some experience in the use of dynamite, write one of the manufacturers and ask for a booklet on the use of dynamite. The manufacturers are required by law to enclose a booklet inside each case of dynamite. A construction company that uses dynamite regularly would probably part with a booklet.

Modern-day dynamiting is now a pretty sophisticated business. The era of the manual blast via the use of fuses is fast vanishing from the construction scene. Manual caps have been replaced with electric blasting caps. Electric-caps are detonated by an electrical charge passing from a storage battery through an insulated electric cord to the caps. The concussion created by the detonated caps causes the dynamite to explode.

With the use of electric caps, there is a "fail-safe" method of reducing the chances of an accident. This involves the use of a galvanometer. A galvanometer is an instrument which measures small amounts of electrical current. In its application to using dynamite, the galvanometer has two poles at its base. We touch the ends of the two wires that are encased in the detonating cord individually, but at the same time, one to each pole at the base of the galvanometer. If you have a good connection, the needle on the galvanometer will arc to the right of the gauge and indicate its maximum reading. If the needle does not get into the maximum zone or does not show any reading at all, then you have a poor connection or unconnected wire. In either case it is unsafe to attempt to detonate the charge. You then must check the detonating cord for breaks in it; also check the cord all the way to the charge because one of the electric blasting cap wires may have become disconnected or broken. If the detonating cord is broken, it's easily spliced. If a blasting cap wire is broken, a new cap should be installed in the "charge." The electrical system then should be rechecked before detonation.

Hardhats should be worn by all individuals in the vicinity of the blast site. It is not uncommon to have small rocks sail a quarter of a mile after the blast. When a rock hits your skin it stings! You should detonate (blast) from behind or under shelter whenever possible.

It's fun to create blind sites with the use of explosives. However, we are doing it with a most powerful form of dangerous energy! To prevent accidents in using explosives takes good organization and the operation must entail the use of the best-known practices. You must remember that you are directing a powerful force. Various safety devices, such as the galvanometer, and other methods are available which will minimize risk exposure.

We cannot contemplate every situation; but we can, from being knowledgeable, know what to do. I suggest that if you are interested in learning more about dynamiting, you write the Institute of Makers of

Explosives, 420 Lexington Avenue, New York, New York 10017. From them you can obtain the following pamphlets: Standard Storage Magazines; American Table of Distances; Rules for Storing; Transporting and Shipping Explosives; Safety in the Handling and Use of Explosives; Radio Frequency Energy — A Potential Hazard in the Use and Transportation of Electric Blasting Caps; Explosives in Agriculture; and How to Destroy Explosives.

Camouflaging the Blinds — Wood Blinds

Once you've got the site cleaned out and the blind assembled, we begin the most important job of camouflaging. The camouflage material must be absolutely as natural as possible. Blinds near tules (cattails) should be camouflaged with tules. The same is true of blinds near salt grass, sagebrush, evergreen trees, etc. When no natural camouflage is available, camouflage netting like the type used on artillery in World War II is fine. Care should be exercised that all loose material is stapled to the wood; otherwise if it's allowed to flap in the breeze, it'll "spook" the birds.

The Actual Camouflaging

The concept in camouflaging is to make everything look as natural as possible. The blind should blend into the surroundings. We can reduce the amount of camouflage necessary by backfilling as much dirt as possible around the exposed portions of the blind. Don't pile the dirt up at such an angle that it's in danger of falling down. Just taper it nicely.

Installed camouflaged Piano Blind

47

Next we drive eight-penny galvanized nails into the corners of each panel. The nails should be allowed to protrude one-half inch so that you can tie wire to them. Use galvanized nails as there is no sheen to them and they won't rust. Tules, salt grass, sagebrush and brush can all be cut with a gas-operated brush cutter. Both McCulloch and Homelite make excellent machines. Retail on a brush cutter runs about $275. The brush cutter will enable you to cut off all the camouflage material right at the roots or stalks.

After you have cut enough camouflage material for a blind, the next step is to apply it. The finished blind should not have too bulky an appearance. If you use brush, break the branches off the stalk or stem so that the branches lie flat when applied. Tules and salt grass, of course, are not a problem because they'll lie flat anyway.

Application of Camouflage

Under my methods, two people can camouflage a blind nicely. If you have four people available, you can work two to a side. You can begin at any corner of a panel. It's easier to start at the top. Tie the end of the wire to the predriven nail. Eighteen-gauge wire or stovepipe wire is fine just so long as it's malleable. Since the wire comes in rolls, after making the tie you can leave the roll at the end of the run.

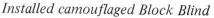

Installed camouflaged Block Blind

One person holds the material in place and the other feeds it to him. Pressure must be kept on the material so it doesn't slip. The person applying the material can keep one hand on the material and pull on the wire with the other. When you've reached the end of the run, stretch the wire as tightly as possible before tying it off. It will also be necessary to drive nails for the middle camouflage run of each panel. When you get through the run, look to see if there are any "holidays." If so just slip a piece of brush or whatever into the void. Two or three tiers of camouflage will finish each panel depending on the material you're using.

Pillbox Blind in process of being camouflaged

All we have left to camouflage is the roof and, in some cases, the door. We'd only have to camouflage the door on Piano Blinds and the modified Piano Blind, floating blind, etc. In the case of any wood-roofed blind, again, drive the galvanized nails into the corners. Lay the camouflage on in runs and tie it off. The material should extend slightly (about four inches) over the shooting edge of the roof. This reduces the amount of actual opening and gives the birds less to look at. After the brush is all tied off by tier, run wires cross fashion from one corner to another; then cinch the wires and tie them.

The door can be camouflaged by driving one six-penny nail in each corner. This should be done carefully so that you don't fracture the wood. Bend the nails over inside the blind so that nobody catches their clothing on them. Tie your wire from one nail to another until the wire forms a square. Cut your brush or whatever down to the size of the door. Then fill up the square created by the wire.

After the first year, simply put new camouflage over the old and you're in business again. When the blind gets too bulky looking, strip some of the old camouflage off and replace it with new material.

Camouflaging the Blind Area

After you're completely done with your blind installation and camouflaging of the blind, get a metal rake and rake the ground area immediately around the blind. Plant the area with grass seed and water it a few times. In rainy areas, repeated watering is, of course, not necessary. In arid areas common grass seed won't survive but various fescue grasses will. I've planted fescue grasses in areas that had less than eight inches annual rainfall and they do fine.

The duck hunter's helper — the gas operated brush cutter. Courtesy Homelite, Port Chester, New York.

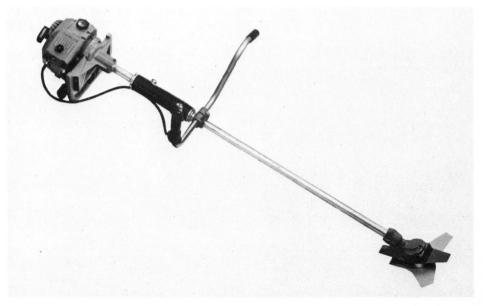

Painting Wood Blinds

As the "shooting face" of the blind is obviously open it will allow the birds to look in. For the birds, the new plywood serves as an excellent background to spot shooters. To rectify this the entire background inside the blind should be painted drab olive or duckboat color. Be sure that the paint is flat not glossy. If you don't have a source of duckboat paint, write Cowman-Campbell Paint Company, 5221 Ballard Avenue N.W., Seattle, Washington 98107. They actually manufacture a brand called "Duckboat Paint."

You can, of course, paint the whole blind but new wood will age drab in one year anyway. Paint however will preserve the wood. Blinds I've installed ten years ago are still in good shape but only by proper care. The door hinges and hook should be sprayed or painted flat black. Every precaution must be taken to avoid spooking the birds.

Camouflaging Rock Blinds

In Chapter 2, it was suggested that wire hoops be placed in the mortared joints while the cement was still wet. Having done this, all you need to do now is cut the material and stick it in the hoops. Each year replace it with fresh camouflage material. Natural rock requires no painting, but circular cesspool blocks or pumice blocks should be painted drab olive. A large piece of brush should be cut to fill in the door opening.

Camouflaging Tank Blinds

This is not too difficult a job as the bulk of the blind is beneath the surface of the water. Prior to installation, the entire blind should be painted with no-sheen black paint. Painting serves two purposes: It prevents rust and camouflages the blind at the same time. After the blind is installed, cut a large enough piece for camouflage netting to cover the top and the exposed sides of the blind. Attach the netting to the hooks welded on the roof. The ends of the netting will hang in the water. Cut several small half-inch saplings and run them into the mud through the camouflage netting. This will prevent the netting from flopping in the wind and spooking the birds. At this point, the tank blind looks like a rock. But you can go one step further and cut a few willow shoots, if available, and spot them around the blind. This breaks up the outline and gives a better appearance. Willow shoots in water will stay green and hold their leaves for several weeks.

Courtesy Eddie Bauer, Inc. Seattle, Washington

Chapter 5
DUCK DECOYS AND SETS

Section I - Decoys

Good duck decoys make up phase two of successful duck hunting. If we're going to get our share of ducks then we must be willing to make an investment in good decoys. We wouldn't consider hunting with an inferior shotgun, so we should have the same high regard for the use of good decoys!

Good decoys, with the proper care and maintenance, should last at least ten years. This represents a small investment for the years of pleasure they will provide.

Types of Decoys

Today's commercial duck decoy is made from one of three materials: plastic, rubber or cork. All three produce excellent lifelike decoys. The three types work well on any type of water. The cork variety may have a slight edge in salt water and heavy seas because of its greater buoyant qualities.

When I say commercial duck decoy I am not excluding the small companies and individuals who still turn out wood decoys. They are excellent craftsmen and produce fine products. Those of you who use wood decoys and have enjoyed success should continue using them.

On the following pages we have pictured several different types of duck decoys. They are all fine decoys and will get the job done.

Section 2 - Decoy Sets

How Many Decoys and Why

For many years great mystery has shrouded the use of decoys and the proper number of them that should be set out. The number of decoys varies with the size of the water you're shooting.

Big Water — Big water takes big stools of decoys. To justify this statement you only have to recall that the ducks raft in big bunches on large bodies of water. For this reason, you should put out as many decoys as is feasible in making your stool. When you're shooting large bodies of water, 100 decoys aren't too many. Large decoy spreads are particularly attractive to small flocks of five birds or less as they decoy much more readily to large stools. Under windy conditions where you have pronounced wave action, the large stool of decoys will also show up better.

Small Potholes — On small potholes, large stools of decoys are not necessary. One-half dozen to a dozen decoys are quite adequate, particularly if you're a good caller. Twenty ducks would be a big flock on a small pothole or pond, so you're just wasting your efforts in putting out a big stool.

Streams — A decoy operation on a stream depends on the size of the stream. If you were shooting the Mississippi, you'd need three or four dozen decoys. Because its big water, the birds have lots of places to go and it's essential to have a large attractive stool. By contrast, on a small creek you can get by with half a dozen decoys.

Fields — When you have the good fortune to find fields the birds are feeding in, decoys put the frosting on the cake. They assure the birds that have been feeding there that everything is okay. Because wheat, pea, barley and cornfields all have stubble or stalks, they are bound to reduce the percentage of decoys that can be seen. For this reason, the decoys should be placed in little open spots so they can be "spotted" easier. You should also use what is known in the trade as a "magnum" decoy which is simply an oversized duck decoy. Some of the magnum decoys come equipped with stakes which allow them to sit off the ground and show up better. In field shooting, you should use at least three dozen duck decoys. All ducks have a rather high regard for the intelligence of a goose. We use this admiration to an advantage by putting three or four goose decoys in with the duck decoys.

Ocean, Bays and Tidal Flats — Oceans, bays and tidal flats all take large stools of decoys. Birds that use these waters have a tendency to raft up in flocks of several thousand and are often hard to decoy. For this reason, the bigger the stool, the greater your success. For example, on Chesapeake Bay, decoy sets of 200 are not uncommon.

Most people are reluctant to put out that many because of the water depths and tide fluctuations. We have devised a method that overcomes both the depths and tide fluctuations which we discuss in "How Much Line" later in this chapter.

The Fallacy of So-called "Patterns"

Down through the years we have all read many stories and have seen many complicated illustrations of decoy patterns. Let me say this about that! Let's imagine that we could eavesdrop on a conversation between the "flight leader" and the rest of a flock of mallards as they depart an Iowa cornfield.

The flight leader says, "All right, boys, today's flight plan calls for our landing at Boulder Lake in a fishhook pattern." Sounds kind of silly doesn't it? Well, it is silly because birds decoy to a stool because they want to. Remember that and you won't go wrong.

In setting out decoys, there is only one important thing to do. Get the birds to come in! We accomplish this by making our decoy set-ups look as natural as possible. Ducks sit on the water in clusters; they are rarely strung out. Knowing this we try to recreate the conditions ducks are most used to.

Birds in landing always pick open spots. To take advantage of this habit, the open spots should occur exactly in front of the blind. By an open spot I mean an opening of at least several yards. We accomplish this by splitting the decoy flock. The opening then occurs right in front of the blind which is where it should be. The farthest decoy should be no more than twenty-five or thirty yards from the blind. The closest decoy should be about seven yards.

Big flocks light away from decoy sets and swim in. If your decoys are set fifty yards from the blind, decoying birds will light seventy yards away which is undesirable. Bring the birds to you; you'll get more!

Pintail Decoys.
Courtesy Neumann & Bennetts, Inc.
Klamath Falls, Oregon

COMMONLY USED DUCK DECOYS.

Mallard Decoys.
Courtesy Herter's Inc.
Waseca, Minnesota

Mallard Decoy.
Courtesy Woodstream Corporation
Lititz, Pennsylvania

Mallard Decoy.
Courtesy Neumann & Bennetts, Inc.
Klamath Falls, Oregon

Mallard and Pintail Decoys.
Courtesy Eddie Bauer, Inc.
Seattle, Washington

Bluebill Decoys.
Courtesy Herter's Inc.
Waseca, Minnesota

Mallard Decoy.
Courtesy Herter's Inc.
Waseca, Minnesota

Teal Decoys.
Courtesy Dye-Call Company
Seattle, Washington

Mallard Decoys.
Courtesy Dye-Call Company
Seattle, Washington

Coastal Decoys made from cork.
Courtesy L.L. Bean Inc.
Freeport, Maine

Wind, Decoys and Blinds

The formula we just discussed is a simple one. It's easy to apply under good conditions. But, let's assume we have some unfavorable conditions like a good brisk wind. In the case of a brisk wind when the blind is not located in a sheltered area, we would modify the split-decoy flock arrangement by moving all of the decoys to one side of the blind.

The wind direction determines this. An example would be, if the wind were blowing from the south, the birds would approach the decoys from the north. The decoys therefore should be placed slightly north of the blind. The opening then occurs in front of the blind and as the birds approach the decoys from the north, they'll light right at the edge of our decoys.

Alternate Blinds in Winds

The situation we just described is fine if the lake lies north and south, but let's compound our problem and say the lake lies east and west. You'd have a problem unless you had blinds on both the north and south sides of the lake.

Decoys and the proper blind for each wind condition go hand in hand. In the example just illustrated, in the lake lying east and west with the wind blowing from the north and the birds decoying from the south, you'd have to shoot the north side in order to get good shooting. If you shot the south side under these conditions, the birds would be coming in from behind you which is not a desirable situation.

On large bodies of water you should have blinds for all wind conditions. If you do this, it's a simple matter to set your decoys up to conform to the wind condition. To assist you in your decoy calculations, a wind table has been printed.

WIND TABLE

Condition	Bird Reaction
North Wind	Birds decoy from the south
South Wind	Birds decoy from the north
East Wind	Birds decoy from the west
West Wind	Birds decoy from the east

South Wind →

Lee Bay

Section 3 - Decoys in Water Variation, Lines and Anchors

How much Line?

Decoys With Keels

The question often arises: How much line should I put on my decoys? The answer is: enough to work in most of the bodies of water you're shooting. Most commercial decoys manufactured today have keels on them. The keels are large enough so that even if you're using braided nylon line, you can get at least forty-five feet wrapped around the keel. Forty-five feet will handle most water.

To adjust the line to the particular water you're shooting, simply drop the anchor into the water. When the anchor hits bottom, make a half hitch with one hand as shown in the illustration. Cinch the line up against one end of the keel, with your other hand pulling it until it's tight. This is known as "keeling" the decoy line.

By keeling the decoy line, this prohibits the line from playing out. If you merely dropped the anchor into the water and had any wind action at all, the line would unwind making a mess of the first magnitude. There are all kinds of devices that are used to hold decoy line and allow the line to fit the situation. But, I feel because of its simplicity, the keeling method works best.

The Anchor Clip

The anchor clip is used with decoys that have partially edged keels. An oval anchor, as shown in the illustration, fits snugly in a space between the partially edged keels. Just flip the anchor out of the bottom clip and unwind enough line to reach the bottom.

Decoys Without Keels

When you're using decoys that don't have keels or don't have solid keels, you can handle the line in several ways.

Body Winding — To body wind the decoy line, tie the line to the decoy, then wrap the line around the center of the body. Be sure you wind it as tightly as possible. When you've finished winding the line around the body, leave enough slack to wrap the remaining line around the head a couple of times.

A variation of body winding is used with shell plastic decoys. There is a lip formed at the end of the decoy between the body edge and the tail. Again tie the line to the decoy, then run it around the lip, back around the head, creating a figure eight. Repeat the figure eight until you've wrapped most of the line, leaving just enough for a couple of loops around the head.

Separated Anchors — Using keelless decoys, there is still another method of handling the anchor and line problem. The anchor, usually an open square of lead, has the line wrapped around the square and is clipped to the rest of the line with a small diaper pin or some other clipping device.

When you're putting out the decoys, you clip the line onto the decoy with the safety pin. Then drop the anchor into the water until it hits bottom. This is only practical in areas where you've measured the water depth. The water depth must also be constant and not fluctuate.

The separated anchor method works quite well. The anchors are carried in a pail and the lineless decoys are sacked up.

Setting Decoys in 400 Feet of Water

Most hunters would lose their dentures at the thought of putting decoys out in 400 feet of water! Actually it's quite simple. 400 feet would be the extreme because most people don't get exposed to this kind of water depth.

But in places like Lake Michigan, the Atlantic and Pacific Oceans and the deeper lakes, you will encounter these deep water situations.

The Solution

The first thing we need is the anchor. Under these conditions we use bricks. We use the old variety as they're easy to come by and the cost is more reasonable. To prepare the brick, take a file and make a ring completely around the middle of the brick. The groove need only be deep enough to hold the decoy line .

For decoy line we use fifteen-pound test monafilament line. We buy this commercially in spools of 5,000 yards. This way it's quite cheap. The next thing you'll need is some plastic fishing floats, bobber-type. They should be about two inches in diameter so they're easy to spot. We spray these with fluorescent paint.

The Application

Tie the line to the brick. Wrap it around several times. Then lower the brick to whatever the depth is. When you've reached the bottom allow five or six feet of slack in the line and slip the float on. The slack is to allow for wind changes and minor water fluctuations. In areas affected by tides, you'll have to make the necessary calculations. If you're shooting a low tide, the fact your floats are submerged at high tide is not a problem.

When you put your decoy on, clip it to the clip on the end of the line and put the float in a bucket. When you're through shooting you take the decoy off and put the float back on. The reason we use fluorescent floats is so that they can be easily spotted. A good lantern or flashlight helps spot them.

The Results

In your willingness to cope with these apparently impossible conditions, a number of things have been accomplished. You're going to have less competition and also less work once you're set up. You can also leave your decoys out permanently if you so desire, in which case you don't need the floats. I'll discuss leaving decoys out permanently later in this chapter.

In the situation we just discussed, your shooting results will be fantastic! A deep water operation generally results in limits everytime. I hit upon the deep water concept several years ago and would now prefer to shoot deep water.

Fast Shallow Water Sets

This method is particularly good on public hunting areas. Some states do not allow decoys to be left out over night or unattended in public areas. But it works well elsewhere! Large spreads of decoys take a considerable length of time to set out and take up.

One system we use for shallow water, water less than ten feet deep, is to set up strings of four decoys and only use two anchors. Look at the illustration "Shallow Water Decoy Set-up" and note our method of tying up these strings of decoys.

The minimum distance between decoys would be that distance that prevents the decoys from touching when they are tail to tail. However, we generally tie the decoys about four feet apart. Using tangle-free decoy line eliminates the need to wrap lines between decoys. The oval-style anchors will hold enough line to reach the bottom, and they will not unwind any unnecessary line.

Setting your decoys out.

Fast Tidal Flat Sets

The same system we just described in "Fast Shallow Water Sets" also works well on tidal flats. When using this anchoring system, leave enough line on the anchor to compensate for the increase of water depth due to incoming tides. The tide will lift the anchor partially off the bottom and it will unwind one more turn and your decoy will still remain in place. Simple isn't it!

Space available — Note split between decoy flock.

61

When you're setting decoys from a boat, using the four-feet-to-a-string system, you can set them out quite rapidly. You can set 100 decoys in ten minutes using two people. You can pick them back up in fifteen to twenty minutes. The secret is to stack the decoys neatly in piles of four as they are taken in. When you pick up, wrap the tangle-free line around the anchor and slip the anchor over the head of the end decoy.

This tangle-free line is good stuff. It remains flexible in below zero degree weather and will hold any knot without tangling or slipping. You can get some by writing Dye-Call Company, 1309 North 77th, Seattle, Washington 98103, and asking for a sample.

Leaving Decoys out Permanently

Putting decoys out everyday can be a great deal of work. This is particularly true if you're dealing with deep water and high winds. You can cut down on your work load by leaving decoys out for prolonged periods of time.

I suggest this method if it complies with your state law. Some states have a law which prohibits leaving decoys out on public lands. This law does not pertain to private property. It was designed to eliminate people from taking "squatter rights" on good spots.

There are some disadvantages to leaving decoys out but they are offset by the advantages. The biggest hazard is theft. However, most good insurance policies cover this, at least the first time. Icing conditions cause

Blinds are directly behind decoy stool.

some problems. You have to allow enough time before shooting time to "dip" the decoys to rinse the ice and frost off. You can do this with a boat oar. In extremely cold weather ice flows are a problem. As the wind changes, the ice flows change also. If you're using monafilament line, the ice will cut the line off leaving your decoys to float away. In a lake you can pick them up later; on a stream they're gone.

Braided nylon line will survive most ice flows if you're using bricks for weights. The bricks will reduce line drag and the ice will usually pass by. You will run into ice flows only in cases of extreme thaws or rapid freezing followed by a quick thaw. In Eastern Washington where I live, you run into this quite frequently. When you leave decoys out under these conditions, you should allow enough time to make repairs before shooting time. I always have extra decoys, bricks and monafilament line along and generally can get functional by shooting time.

Those of you who shoot salt water or live in mild climates, of course, aren't faced with these problems. Ice flows or not, theft or not, I think the pluses out number the minuses when it comes to leaving decoys out.

Decoy Lines

In deep water, monafilament line is the most economical and most practical. In moderately deep water, 15 to 40 feet deep, the braided nylon No. 30 is best. This line was originally developed to repair gill nets used for catching salmon here in the Pacific Northwest. In case you don't have a local source you can get it by writing Nordby Supply Company, 2600 West Commodore Way, Seattle, Washington 98199.

The tangle-free anchor line used in tidal flat sets is the best under any shallow conditions. You may refer to that section for the name and address of the supplier.

Anchors

In deep water we use bricks. However, if you have a cheap source of lead or own a junkyard, almost anything small but reasonably heavy will do the job. Take your pick.

In moderately deep water or shallow water both the common mushroom sinkers and collar anchors work fine. The collar anchors described in our shallow water sets fit right over the decoy's neck and prohibit the line from tangling. If you're interested in saving money, you can buy molds for both the mushroom and collar sinkers and make all you want.

Repair and Maintenance of Decoys

In football the best defense is a good offense. The same application can be made to decoy care. If you handle decoys gingerly and avoid throwing them around, they'll last longer. If you practice this you'll eliminate much of your decoy maintenance. Throwing decoys causes most of the fractures we find on decoy seams. Carry the decoys to shore rather than throw them!

The number two offender in decoy cripplings is the "sluicer." Some people like to sluice birds. These are the "meat men." Some sluicing is justified if you have a cripple. At least let the bird swim out of the decoys before you shoot it.

To repair decoys that have been shot or have fractured seams, any good epoxy glue will do the job. Drain the water out by tilting the decoy. In some cases it may be necessary to enlarge the pellet hole which will speed up the draining process. Dry the damaged portion and apply epoxy glue. After the glue has dried for several days, touch the decoy up with its respective colors. Make sure the paint you apply is no-sheen so as not to spook the birds. From a practical standpoint, it's better to repair several decoys at one time than to repair them one at a time.

Shallow water decoy set.

Set decoy in half the time as required with single anchored decoys. Use 2 special over-the-head anchors and attach 4 decoys, as shown. Your set will stay in place regardless of weather. When picking up your set, wrap tangle free anchor line around anchors and slip anchor over the head of end decoy. Line between decoys may be left unwound – it won't tangle or knot when placed in boat or decoy bag.

The anchor clip.
Courtesy Dye-Call Company
Seattle, Washington

Keeling a decoy.

Chapter 6
DUCK CALLING
AND CALLS

In the practice of quackery it pays to be a perfect fake! Most ducks will respond to the mallard call. Female ducks do the calling and most female ducks, regardless of species, sound much the same. Mallard drakes make a low-pitched gabble while Pintails, Widgeon and other drakes make a whistling sound. Some ducks, like Wood Ducks for instance, make a very high-pitched squeal but live in the same area as Mallards and will fly with them.

For the beginner, duck calling is often a hit-or-miss affair. Very few people have the time or opportunity to study ducks enough to understand the reason for the sounds they make. The long-gone market hunter often used as many as a dozen different calls. He may not have had names for each sound but he knew how to make them and when to use each one. He thought like a duck. After forty years of hunting and studying ducks and several years of teaching duck calling classes we can recommend a system of learning to aid the beginner.

Instead of a dozen sounds to learn we can break down duck calling to only four different sounds that can be learned much easier. Once the student has mastered these four calls he can and will add variations to them as his experience grows. Many duck hunters begin their hunting experience by jump shooting. This method puts the beginner in the field for the least amount of expense. If the jump shooter then decides to use decoys and a duck call, he often makes the only sound of the duck call that he has heard. The experienced hunter realizes that the sound made by ducks as they are jumped from a resting or feeding area is the alarm sound. Listen to the next duck you jump and you'll hear this distress cry. It can be heard for many hundreds of yards and will alert all ducks within hearing range. The ducks will then know that danger is lurking. The alarm sound is the most common mistake made on the duck call by the beginner. Just what is an alarm sound? Anytime you start a low-pitched call and progress to higher and higher pitched quacks on your duck call, you are making the alarm sound. Please don't practice this call. It's too easy to make.

Play the recording that we have furnished with this book. We have given the four basic calls to aid the beginner. Real, live duck sounds are also on the record to provide you with the sounds you'll be trying to imitate in your duck calling.

To produce the reedy sound of the Mallard duck, the air must come from the diaphragm — that is take a deep breath and push the air through the call with the diaphragm. Hold your hand on the stomach area as you blow — if you can not feel movement, you are blowing from the throat and the sounds will not be effective enough. To produce the quack of the Mallard, the magic word is "HOOT." Practice saying this word and hold your hand in the area of the stomach. You will notice the muscles contract and stop as the word "HOOT" is ended. Use the same action in producing the quack in your duck call. This may seem strange at first but good singers do it as well as all ducks. You can do it too! To increase the volume/pitch of your tone, merely increase the air pressure going through the call — that is, say the magic word "HOOT" louder.

Herter's Gloda Duck Call.
Courtesy Herter's Inc.
Waseca, Minnesota

Olt "99" Duck Call.
Courtesy P.S. Olt Company
Pekin, Illinois

Faulk's Champion Duck Call.
Courtesy Faulk's Game Call Company
Lake Charles, Louisiana

Dye's Mallard Call.
Courtesy Dye-Call Company
Seattle, Washington

Herter's Vit-Gloda Duck Call.
Courtesy Herter's Inc.
Waseca, Minnesota

Olt Mark V Duck Call.
Courtesy P.S. Olt Company
Pekin, Illinois

The position of the hand holding the call is very important — the correct position is to hold the call by the very tip between the thumb and forefinger. Holding the call in this position will allow the other three fingers and the palm of the hand to act as a "bellmouth" for your call in much the same manner used with musical instruments. Opening and closing the hand, will vary the tone from a muted to a full tone. We have illustrated the proper hand position to hold your call.

To better understand the record, we have printed a pictorial sketch of each call with pitch, volume and time in seconds. If you will now relate this to the record as it plays, the audio portions emphasizing each of the four calls will correspond to the call charts we have printed on the following pages.

This eight-minute record and the call charts we have illustrated here will actually enable you to get in the duck calling business. To obtain proficiency it takes practice, practice and more practice; but it pays off. Time and again we have successfully called ducks right out of other duck blinds, not because their calling was inferior but because ours was better. Good callers are like athletes, they take years of development.

Reams have been written about different types of duck calls. Generally, calls fall into two distinct categories: plastic reed or metal reed. The plastic reed call is by far the most common due to ease of manufacturing. Occasionally plastic reeds "stick" if they have become damp from blowing. It's a good idea to carry an extra call to assure having a dry one to work the next flock with. Some of the accomplished callers use metal reeds extensively. For the beginner we feel a plastic reed call is a little easier to learn on. Once the caller has developed his diaphragm muscles to control his calling, he can change to a metal reed call very satisfactorily. Spring-tempered bronze seems to make the best metal reeds and once tuned, they will remain tuned for many years. Metal reed calls usually have an excellent resistance to dampness and very stable tone range.

In summarizing the duck calling chapter, we have hit all of the high points on duck calling and calls. The important thing about the call is you feel comfortable. Be it a plastic reed call or metal reed call, you're the one who has to use it. Pick a good one. At the end of this chapter we have pictured several duck calls. Any one of them properly used will do the job. The call charts and record will give you the opportunity to learn duck calling as the "pros" do it.

My co-author on this chapter, Harry Dye, is a modest individual, but I won't miss this opportunity to suggest that you get his long-play forty-minute record. His LP is the condensation of his six-hour duck calling class which he gives in various Western States. You can obtain the record by writing Harry Dye, Dye-Call Company, 1309 North 77th, Seattle, Washington 98103.

Holding the call in the proper position.

THE HAIL OR HIGHBALL CALL

Use this call when the ducks are more than 300 yards out from your blind. This call will generally be the first call used to attract the attention of passing ducks. Repeat the HAIL call over, and over until it becomes apparent that the flock is turning toward you or until the birds are out of calling range. The first quarter second note "qu" can be left out if it causes a problem; however, using this note helps to pace the volume/pitch and the timing.

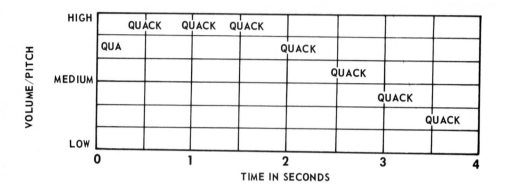

THE GREETING OR COMEBACK CALL

Once you have turned a flock of ducks it is apparent that they are interested in your calling. After the highball has attracted the flock and they have come within 300 yards of your blind, change over to the greeting or comeback call. Use this call until the ducks are within 100 yards. This call is much like the highball except it is more excited and pleading, but has less pitch/volume. Do not call when the ducks are coming straight toward you as they may see your movements and this will cause them to flare away.

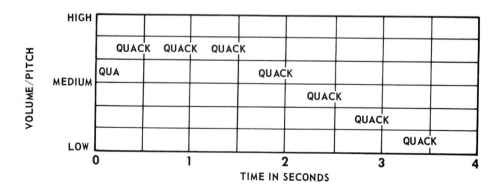

THE FEED CALL

The feed call is the third call to be used and it probably will be the most important call of all. To make the feed call, the word is "TICK TICK TICK" in a very rapid movement of the tongue - some callers prefer to use the word "KITTY KITTY KITTY." Use this call when the ducks are within 150 yards or closer. Generally the feed call is used when a flock has just passed overhead or very close to the blind. Feed calls are sounds of contentment and may be heard from ducks inflight or on the water. Always answer a feed call with a feed call.

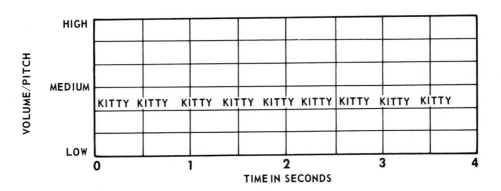

THE LONESOME HEN CALL

The lonesome hen call is primarily a call to attract ducks already on the water. Making this call is by a slow series of simple "quacks" of medium low volume/pitch. Space between each quack will equal the time required for each quack. Use this call any time ducks are on the water and out of range of your blind. Feed calls can be interspersed with the lonesome hen call to make it more effective.

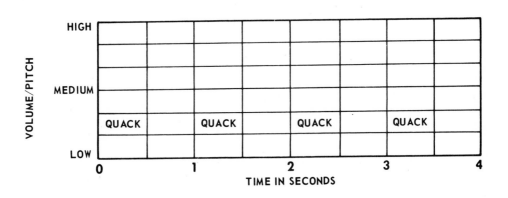

Central Flyway

GEESE

A goose represents the rebel in all of us and because they're wild and free, they have a certain quality that shines out and makes us wish that we were not bound to labor in life, but rather that we could drift as they do with the seasons.

May 1, 1972 Paul S. Bernsen

Publisher's Note

The Les C. Kouba masterful paintings of wild geese which follow are from the collection of Eddie Bauer Expedition Outfitter and the originals are on display at Bauer headquarters in Seattle, Washington.

The reproductions are printed here with sincere thanks to them for their valuable contribution to this book.

Albert P. Salisbury, President
Superior Publishing Company

COURTESY OF EDDIE BAUER

Chapter 7
GEESE

The five most important species of geese to the waterfowler in North America are the Canada Goose, the Lesser Canada, the Snow Goose, the Blue Goose and the White-fronted (Specklebelly). Of the five, the Blue Goose and the Specklebelly are the least known to the U.S. and Canadian gunners. The Blue and Specklebelly are peculiar to particular areas and most hunters never get a chance at them. The exception to this is the shooter who hunts them as they are migrating from their breeding grounds or has an opportunity to hunt them on their wintering grounds.

The Lesser Canada and Snow Goose have much broader coverage and are much better known. If anything, they are becoming more familiar, even on flyways they once used lightly. This proves their adaptability to new conditions — habitat, agricultural changes and population expansions.

The Canada Goose has almost emerged as a national figurehead. He is a familiar sight to shooters almost everywhere in the U.S. and Canada. In addition to his broad range and wide distribution, his numbers are actually on the increase. This has been reflected in longer seasons and increased bag limits.

Wildlife management has done a good job in bringing the Canada Goose "back." The Canada Goose has done well for two reasons: federal and state game refuges have been created and with these came the enforcement of stricter hunting regulations; also contributing to their increase is their breeding range. Because they breed in the extreme north, man has not yet caused any problems in their breeding habitat. It's encouraging to see the increases. It is to be hoped that the lordly Canada Goose can continue to hold its own.

On the following pages we'll do a brief sketch on each of these birds.

The Canada Goose

The common Canada Goose actually has the peculiarity of having both larger and smaller subspecies of itself. The larger being the Giant Canada Goose and the principal smaller ones are the Lesser Canada and Cackler. Here we'll discuss the common Canada Goose.

The Canada Goose with its distinctive cheek patches, majestic wingspan and familiar honk is widely known and widely loved. Whoever does his public relations work has done a fantastic job. Unlike various automobiles, he's always in style and ever popular.

His wariness and built-in intuitions would make James Bond proud. Because of his wariness and ability to anticipate every situation, people have spent more time with a lower ratio of success than when shooting any other form of waterfowl. The man who coined the phrase, "A wild goose chase," wasn't too far from being wrong.

The common Canada Goose or Honker is the second largest North American goose. The largest is the Giant Canada which gets up to eighteen pounds according to ornithologists. The actual average weight of Honkers is between eight and eleven pounds. In thirty-two years of goose hunting, I've shot hundreds of geese and been around thousands more. Of all those geese shot, several dozen weighed eleven pounds. Only a handful weighed more than eleven pounds. Of these, four reached thirteen pounds; two of these I shot myself.

The Canada Goose possesses both exceptional vision and acute hearing. Like most birds, his vision is monocular, as the eyes are located on the sides of the head. Because of this, the birds operate like radar scanning both the horizon and immediate area by moving their heads. Some people might doubt the veracity of hearing about their acute hearing capabilities, but I can vouch for it. In stalking geese, I sometimes crawl several hundred yards. I don't like to crawl with a loaded gun. When I've gotten within a couple hundred yards, I stop and let the birds settle down. At this point, I slip a couple of shells into the chamber. Many times the birds flush from the loading noise. I'd say this was acute enough hearing!

Honkers are primarily vegetarians but will eat shellfish, snails and insects occasionally. On the breeding grounds they eat various aquatic growths, pond lilies, salt grass, cheetgrass, sago plant and almost anything green and tender. In migration, they eat barley, wheat, corn, potatoes, alfalfa and pasture grass in addition to various wild grasses and plants.

Canada geese normally mate for life, but when one dies they will re-mate. Their dedication to each other has often caused the death of both. Many times I've seen one of a pair shot fatally and the survivor will fly around for twenty or thirty minutes, crying mournfully over its loss. In breeding their average production is five. Both parents are proud and devoted and share in the responsibility of raising and safeguarding their brood. The Canada, with its wide range and distribution, also has a wide breeding range. Most of its breeding is done in the Canadian Provinces, Alaska, Labrador, the Yukon and the Northwest Territories. Some Canadas breed in the Western States of Washington, Idaho, Oregon, Montana, the Dakotas and northern California.

Canadian geese are long-lived. In captivity they've lived between thirty and forty years. However, in the wild, twenty-five years would probably be an old bird. There are too many predators, including hunters, that shorten their life span.

Under today's hunting conditions, a Canada Goose has to be regarded as a trophy. To me it takes considerably more know-how to bag a goose than it does some big animals. Many waterfowl hunters have hunted their entire life and have never had the good fortune to get one. I feel very fortunate because I live in an area which is in the heart of their migration flyway. I've shot my share and enjoyed many thrills. But the most important thing is that I've developed a deep admiration for the Canada Goose. In getting to know the bird, I'd say he has considerably more strength of character than some of the people hunting him.

The Lesser Canada Goose

The Lesser Canada, or Lesser as he is referred to, has basically the same identification and characteristics as his cousin, the Canada Goose. The only difference in identification of the two birds is the Lesser's smaller size and shorter neck. A mature Lesser weighs between five and seven pounds.

His calls or honks are similar to the "Honker's" but much more shrill. He also "talks" considerably more than the "Honker" particularly in flight. In decoying or landing into another flock, Lessers make a "droning" sound which is quite distinctive. They also wave from side to side in landing and don't seem to possess the fluid motions of the Canada.

Although he enjoys good vision and the same keen hearing as the "Honker," he obviously lacks the "Honker's" intelligence. Lessers decoy much more readily than "Honkers." Nationally, I'd say there are seven Lessers shot for each "Honker."

Lessers do not have the wide distribution of the Canadas and are better known in the West. They breed primarily in Alaska, the Yukon and the Northwest Territories. They winter mostly in the coastal Western States of Washington, Oregon and California. Arizona, Nevada, New Mexico and Mexico get some winter populations.

The Lesser is a fine table bird and because of inexperience, he is frequently classified as a "Honker" by the novice.

The Snow Goose

There are actually two Snow geese: the Greater and the Lesser. There is little difference between them except for size. They both have the same markings. The bulk of their bodies are white. The wings are two-thirds white except for the tips. The primary feathers on the wing tips are black. Their bills are pink and their heads are "frosted" with a light touch of reddish-brown feathers. Their feet are reddish-pink.

Lesser Snows weigh four-and-a-half to five pounds at maturity while Greater Snows weigh up to seven-and-a-half pounds at maturity. Lesser Snows have a much broader range than the Greater Snows. They breed in Alaska, the Northwest Territories, Upper Hudson Bay and Baffin Island. They winter mainly in California, Texas, Louisiana and Mississippi. With the coming of the vast irrigation projects in Washington, Oregon, Idaho and California, their migratory flyway has drastically changed and birds are getting farther and farther inland. Agriculture and creation of new reservoirs are the chief contributing factors.

The Greater Snow Goose has a much more limited range, breeding in the Baffin Island vicinity as well as the Greenland Coast. It winters in the Carolinas, Virginia, Delaware and lightly in New Jersey.

Both the Greater and Lesser Snow geese are not known for swift mental intelligence. In fact, in many instances, they have outward manifestations of stupidity. Both will decoy to newspapers, toilet tissue, etc., when placed in feeding areas.

The Cree Indians of James Bay call them in orally and have achieved a high degree of skill with their calling. In the more sophisticated decoy operations, good Snow Goose decoys and good calls will pull them in. Snow geese, like the rest of the goose family, love grasses but eat rice, wheat and barley when available.

The Blue Goose

The Blue Goose is a plentiful goose but is only familiar to a very small percentage of hunters. Their limited breeding range and limited wintering range expose them to a handful of shooters. The Blue Goose breeds primarily in the Baffin Island, Upper Hudson Bay and Northwest Territory areas.

It winters in the Louisiana and Texas marshes. It's in migration that the bulk of the birds are shot. The James Bay area is a favorite because it is the first spot where the birds are subjected to any gun pressure. Gunners in Louisiana and Texas do quite well on wintering flocks. The rest of the Blues are shot as migrants as they stop to rest and feed.

Blues are commonly found with Snows and Canadas and readily decoy to all types of goose decoys. Blues weigh five-and-a-half pounds at maturity. They are identified by their white head and neck. The bill, like the Snow Goose's, is pinkish. The body is brownish-gray which gives it an ashy-blue cast. The rump is white with flecks of blue-gray. It can be distinguished from the Emperor Goose by its white neck, as the Emperor Goose's neck is dusky-gray in front and white in back. The Blue, like the Snow Goose, has pinkish feet.

The Blue is an excellent bird to hunt and a James Bay hunt of Blues, Snows and Canadas makes an excellent blend of waterfowl shooting.

The White-Fronted Goose (Specklebelly)

The White-Fronted, or Specklebelly as he is more commonly known, is similar to the Blue Goose in that he is known only to a limited number of shooters. This is because of his breeding range and wintering areas. The Specklebelly breeds in Alaska, the Yukon, the Northwest Territories and Greenland. He winters in Texas and Louisiana but his heaviest winter distribution is in Mexico, California, Washington and Oregon.

He's a familiar bird to West Coast gunners and provides lots of good shooting, particularly in California. The Specklebellies that breed in Greenland provide shooting while in migration to Texas and Louisiana. The Specklebelly, like Blue and Snow geese, is very gregarious and will decoy readily to all goose decoys. They'll also respond to Canada Goose calls.

The Specklebelly's body is mostly brown. Its head has a white band around the front which touches the bill. The lower portion of the breast and undercarriage are white-flecked with black feathers. The rump is gray-white and the feet are yellow.

It's an excellent bird to eat. A mature male Specklebelly weighs slightly more than five pounds, with the female weighing less.

Chapter 8
GOOSE DECOYS, LINES AND ANCHORS

Field Decoys for Geese

There are several types of field decoys: nest-type, full-bodied, folding and silhouette. They all get the job done.

Nest-type Goose Decoys

Nest-type decoys are probably the most popular goose decoy for field shooting. We can attribute this to their light weight and portability. They are designed to nest together for easy handling. Both the heads and stakes are detachable and are easily assembled on location. Their cost is within the range of any goose hunter.

Originally, nest-type decoys were only available in Canada Goose variety. But now both Canada Goose and Snow Goose are available. In both species, the heads are provided in either feeding or sentinel positions.

Full-bodied Goose Decoys

Full-bodied goose decoys are another popular field decoy. They are not as widely used because of their bulk and additional cost. They are as effective as nest-type decoys but are harder to transport.

Full-bodied decoys are among the most lifelike of all goose decoys. Their heads are also detachable and they are staked out by means of a wooden dowel which goes into the base of the decoy.

Folding Goose Decoys

Folding goose decoys have been around a long time. They fold flat but assume a full-bodied effect when their spreader is adjusted in place. A heavy-duty metal stake supports them in the field. As they are made from waterproof fiberboard, they'll last a long time. These decoys are actual photographic reproductions and have a good lifelike quality. They are available in both Canada Goose and Snow Goose.

Silhouette Goose Decoys

Silhouette decoys are probably the oldest form of decoy used to deceive geese. As we know, a silhouette represents a profile. The image of the goose is only projected at certain angles. It's important that they are properly set up so the birds can see them.

The two most common silhouette decoys are made from different materials: weather-resistant plastic and fiberboard. I say most common because both types are commercially manufactured.

The present commercial silhouettes are excellent replicas of the ones we used to spend hours making and painting. Their heads are adjustable to feeding and sentinel positions. The stakes are detachable for transporting.

Many old goose hunters still prefer to make their own silhouettes. They still work, so why not!

Water Decoys for Geese

There are several different floating goose decoys, but only two basic types: a solid-state floating goose decoy and a removable flotation cell variety. Both versions are excellent and get the job done. There are many variations of both types and we will not attempt to discuss them here.

I have rather strong feelings for floating goose decoys as I believe that geese decoy more readily over water as compared to field. I personally have shot hundreds of geese over the last thirty years, most of them over water. I believe that geese don't have the fears and inhibitions near water that they seem to possess in field shooting. I'll go into this in depth in Chapter 10.

Decoy Lines and Anchors
Decoy Lines

Goose decoy line has to be more substantial than duck decoy line because a goose decoy is larger and occupies more surface area. The larger the surface area, the more stress the decoy line will be exposed to. There are several good decoy lines on the market. The braided nylon varieties are excellent.

I personally use nylon parachute cord. It's very stout and lasts well. Like braided nylon line, it's almost impossible to tangle yet it holds knots. There are only a few sources of parachute cord and it takes some looking around to find.

Decoy Anchors

As in the case of decoy line, the anchor will also be under lots of stress. If you use too light an anchor and the decoy is exposed to much wind, then the decoy is going to drift. This isn't a desirable situation because not only will the decoy drift out of the set, which will affect decoying birds, but it might drift completely away.

Therefore, it's important to use heavy anchors. In deep water bricks are good. The application is the same as we discussed in deep water sets for ducks. Oval anchors or "collars" which slip right over the decoy's head are also good. Mushroom-type weights individually are not heavy enough, but three or four of them tied together are okay. The important thing is to anchor the decoy firmly in place and have it stay there.

Nest-type Canada Goose Decoy.
Courtesy Woodstream Corporation
Lititz, Pennsylvania

Nest-type Snow Goose Decoy.
Courtesy Woodstream Corporation
Lititz, Pennsylvania

Folding goose decoy.
Courtesy Wm. R. Johnson Company
Seattle, Washington

Full-bodied goose decoy.
Courtesy Neumann & Bennetts, Inc.
Klamath Falls, Oregon

Full-bodied goose decoys with heads in various positions.
Courtesy Herter's Inc.
Waseca, Minnesota

Floating goose decoy.
Courtesy Herter's Inc.
  Waseca, Minnesota

Silhouette goose decoy in wheat stubble field.

Full-bodied goose decoy in actual use.
Courtesy Neumann & Bennetts, Inc.
  Klamath Falls, Oregon

Chapter 9
GOOSE CALLING AND CALLS

Goose calling requires the ultimate in perfection. In duck calling you can make the occasional faux pas and get away with it; not so with goose calling.

Learning to call geese is much easier than learning to call ducks. There are less notes to learn and geese respond to fewer calls. It's considerably easier to teach someone who has never blown a goose call than to teach a person who has used one. The complete novice has no built-in mistakes. There are two important calls: the highball and the conversation babble.

The Highball

A goose highball call is the sound generally heard from geese as they fly overhead. Most species of geese make the same type of sound, only it varies slightly in pitch. Big Canadian geese are the lowest in pitch and Lesser Canadas, Snows, Blues and other species are slightly higher pitched. All geese will respond to a Honker highball if it's done properly.

Highball Calling

To make your calling easier, select a goose call that fits your requirements. Then practice as much as possible. To start a call, start with low breath pressure and build up your sound volume and air pressure simultaneously until the call "breaks." Hold this sound briefly and cut the note off sharply. This should cause the pitch to break high and create a broken "Hoo-onk." In actual use repeat this sound until the geese respond and turn your way.

The Conversation Babble

The conversation babble is actually four brief "Ho-onks." Each "Ho-onk" has two distinct notes. Decoying geese come in with much fanfare and you should call as excitedly as possible. The conversation babble should be used once you have attracted geese toward your decoy set. Then step up your calling pace and double-note your calls.

If there are others shooting and they are proficient enough to call, have them join in the chorus. Multi-calling if done properly lends to the credibility of the situation.

Dispersing the Sound

When the geese are within 150 yards, it's time to disperse the sound. Hold one hand at the end of the call so that it forms a cross with the hand holding the call. This free hand, slightly cupped, can then be pivoted slowly from side to side which throws the call to one side and then the other. Continue this method of calling, gradually reducing the volume as they approach. Look closely and when the geese are inside your farthest decoy, they're in range.

If you practice these two calls, your shooting success will increase quite sharply. None of us ever seem to get enough practice calling in actual waterfowl shooting so I suggest you get a good goose calling record and listen and practice. There are several goose calling records on the market. Both Faulk's and Herter's have goose calling instructional records in their catalogs.

Calls

Good goose calls are a highly essential part of your goose hunting success. Unless you place a very low value on your time, I'd suggest you invest in a good one. A couple of dollars *will* make a difference in your success. The call you get should be comfortable to you. Some calls can be blown easier than others and if you have any respiratory difficulties you should get one that's easy on your system. Some calls have the "tricks" built right into them, while others require your activating them with your own personal knowledge. Try several and get one that suits you.

Types of Calls

There are many good calls on the market, all made from three basic materials: wood, plastic and rubber. It would be impossible to illustrate and catalog every call manufactured. You, of course, may have your own personal preference. The ones shown here are all excellent calls.

Herter's Saskatchewan Goose Call.
Courtesy Herter's Inc.
Waseca, Minnesota

Herter's Numara Goose Call.
Courtesy Herter's Inc.
Waseca, Minnesota

Faulk's Snow and Blue Goose Call.
Courtesy Faulk's Game Call Company
Lake Charles, Louisiana

Olt "77" Goose Call.
Courtesy P.S. Olt Company
Pekin, Illinois

Chapter 10
GOOSE HUNTING

To hunt a goose is to have lived! To expand on this brief sentence would take a volume in itself. A goose is the Cadillac of all waterfowl. Their extreme wariness and inbred suspicions make them the ultimate challenge in waterfowl hunting. As a small boy the clarion calls from a flock of passing geese aroused more emotion in me than almost anything else could! Even today the calling of a flock of geese will cause me to stop whatever I'm doing and gaze skyward. It's almost as if they were inviting me to join them and many times I wish I could have.

I've hunted geese under every conceivable condition. I've laid on my back in a snowdrift waiting for them to come. I've wrapped myself in green undertaker cloth and made believe I was part of a winter wheat field. Many times I've sat in a goose pit in minus 25° weather and my fingers would get so cold I couldn't feel the trigger when the geese finally came.

I've also stalked them and caught them flat-footed and red-faced and sometimes a lone single has come crying out that it has just lost its mate and I've never cracked a cap because, maybe another time, I'll meet that goose when the odds are even.

In today's era of modern waterfowl management, geese are actually on the increase in many flyways. Widely disbursed federal and state refuges in the U.S., along with the wonderful work Ducks Unlimited has done on the breeding grounds in preserving and improving waterfowl habitat, have saved a valuable resource and preserved a priceless heritage — goose hunting!

The Most Commonly Hunted Geese

Today's most frequently hunted geese are the Canada Goose, Lesser Canada Goose, Snow Goose, Blue Goose and Specklebelly. The methods we are about to describe, if practically applied, will work on all five birds, as well as most of the other species of geese.

Water Blinds

The water blinds we've described and illustrated for ducks work just as well for geese. If you have effectively installed and camouflaged them, they should pass inspection even by a goose. A goose for the most part sticks to large bodies of water — lakes, rivers and tidal bays. Spits, peninsulas and sheltered bays are excellent blind locations.

Geese spend much more time on shorelines and grassy meadows than ducks do. Because of this habit, blinds adjacent to these resting areas will produce geese. If you're going to be a successful goose hunter, then you should spend as much time as possible observing what they do and where they do it. This gives you a little insight to their water habits and helps in selecting blind locations.

Shooting Geese Over Water

Shooting geese over water as opposed to field shooting has a certain magic to it! It has lots of frustrations, but it also offers its share of rewards. In order to successfully shoot geese over water, there is one fundamental to remember: Don't put too much pressure on the geese. If the geese are pressed too hard they'll leave your area and find another more peaceful spot. Even at the height of the migration you shouldn't shoot the same water more than twice a week.

The Best Time to Shoot

In shooting geese over water, the best time to hunt them is when *they return* from feeding. When you find a lake or some other body of water the geese are using, watch them for a couple of days. You can almost set your watch on their takeoff time. Just after dawn they'll start gabbling, then an excited roar and a flock will lift off. Other flocks will follow until the lake is empty. If you shoot at these geese as they go out to feed, most of them won't come back.

Instead of shooting geese as they go out to feed, wait until the last flock has left the lake then leisurely put out your decoys and get your geese when they return. As soon as you've got your birds, pick up your decoys and scat. Geese usually will stay out feeding for two to three hours. Sometimes you can limit in an hour and be gone. Then let the lake rest for three or four days. With rotation shooting you can have sustained good shooting for most of the season or at least until they leave. With this type of waterfowl management, we sometimes have 15,000 migrant geese using our property. But, we never molest them when the area is being rested, not even to shoot ducks.

Goose Decoy Sets in Water

Geese believe there's safety in numbers. In other words, you can't have too many goose decoys. You're restricted only to the number you can put out and take in in a reasonable time. Just as with duck decoy sets, the decoy flock should usually be split so that the opening occurs in front of the blind. A few stake-out decoys on shore supplements the rest of the flock.

In brisk wind conditions you should utilize the wind table we printed in Chapter 5. The table will enable you to place your goose decoys in the proper relation to the blind.

Floating goose decoys should be continually checked for defects. Defective ones should be repaired or discarded. One bad decoy can spook a whole flock. New decoys should be checked for "sheen." If they have any glare at all, put some lampblack on them so they look "flat" in color.

Field Shooting

Field shooting takes lots of effort but it can be very productive. You must also be highly organized and willing to take time to "spot" the fields the geese are feeding in. Field shooting requires more "bird watching" than any other form of goose hunting. By bird watching I mean following the flock until they light in a field and start feeding. To be an effective bird watcher you have to know something about a goose's habits.

Goose Habits in Feeding

Geese normally feed twice a day, morning and evening. They leave their resting areas shortly after dawn on their morning run. On their afternoon feeding cycle they generally leave late in the afternoon, allowing themselves two or three hours for feeding time.

Fog may delay their morning departure time and wind will shorten the distance they're willing to fly to feed. On rainy days they'll stay out feeding most of the day, eliminating the afternoon run. On moonlight nights they'll take off just before dark and feed all night long, returning just before dawn.

These hints will give you a little insight on *when* to watch for them.

What Geese Feed On

A goose is a vegetarian. He likes grains and grasses. In his summer environment in Canada, the Arctic Circle and the Northwest Territories, he eats sago plant, widgeon grass, spike rush, bullrushes, salt grass, cheet grass, mustard grass and cattail shoots.

Migrant geese are largely dependent on modern agriculture. Their first love is barley. Rice and wheat are second choices and corn, oats and rye round out the grains they consume. As far as grains are concerned a goose eats the grain that is available in the area he is passing through. On his southern migration, a goose might start out eating Canadian wheat and end up wintering on California white rice. He has a deep love for grasses. Green winter wheat is a favorite. He also likes the tender pasture grasses. As a grazer he does a better job than any livestock, even sheep.

Alfalfa is okay with geese if the stocks are young and tender. Here in the West, in a country that only gets 8 inches of moisture a year, rain is a luxury. Every couple of years we get some fall rains. This causes cheetgrass seeds to germinate. They produce very tender shoots which the geese love. It is a strange sight to see hundreds of geese lighting in the sagebrush.

Goose Spotting

Most people don't hunt by themselves and goose "watching" is more effectively done in teams. Two or more people should split about a mile apart and watch the birds as they leave the refuge or lake they're using. A good pair of binoculars is a prerequisite. When the geese start taking off, watch them as long as possible, then drive to the point you last saw them. Other flocks will follow the first batch and from your new position follow them. You'll soon have the field they're feeding in pinpointed. Don't bother them, just let them feed. The distance you drive will vary each time as geese will keep feeding farther and farther away. This is because they move as soon as fields are "fed-out."

The reason for more than one "spotter" is to assure that the geese don't slip out unnoticed. If you spend much time field shooting you'll always know what general area the geese are feeding in.

"Pitting In"

Earlier I said, "Don't bother the geese while they're feeding." This is an excellent rule as geese will use the same field for several days if they are not bothered.

Before digging pits, be sure to get the owner's permission. If the property isn't leased this is usually not too difficult. Assure him you'll fill the pits in as soon as you're through using them.

Camouflaged Pit Blind on water edge.

The Pits

When I use the word "pits" it's all encompassing and covers everything from wheat field pits to pits in alfalfa. The pit should be dug after the birds have finished feeding. If you've spotted the birds in the morning, dig the pit after they leave. If it's an afternoon feeding, the pit should be dug at night.

In Chapter 2, we have discussed pits rather extensively so the actual pit construction and camouflaging can be taken from that text. It's important to get rid of the dirt that comes out of the pit. It should not be scattered. Scattered dirt shows up as a fresh circle from the air. Part of the dirt can be banked up around the pit and covered with straw. The rest should be hauled away and returned later when you fill the pit in.

In some states geese can only be hunted on a "jump date" basis. In Washington we can only shoot geese on Wednesdays, Saturdays, Sundays and holidays. If your state works similarly, you may be restricted on how soon you can shoot from the pit you've just dug.

In any event, you should shoot the pit as soon as possible — in fact the same day if you dug it in the morning. The weather might change, forcing the geese to migrate, or they might move to another field. The old adage "A goose in the hand" is a good one.

Field Decoy Tips

To have a good decoy operation you need at least 100 decoys. The decoys can be left in the pits which eliminates hauling them back and forth. If you leave them in the pits, clean them with fresh rags from time to time and get the dirt off.

Early in the season when the geese aren't spooky, silhouettes work fine. But later, when the birds are more wary, you should have some full-bodied decoys mixed in with the silhouettes. If you can afford it you should use as many full-bodied decoys as possible. When I say full-bodied I am including nest-type and folding goose decoys.

A flock of geese about to decoy.
Courtesy George Leonard Herter

The Sets

Because the decoys are on land they take a little more meticulous setting than water sets. Water flotation will cure some decoy irregularities, but on land the decoys must be absolutely perfect.

Geese, like ducks, land into the wind. They also feed into the wind. With that in mind, the decoys should be pointed headfirst into the wind. Your pattern can be a split flock with the opening occurring in front of the pit or pits. The decoy stakes should be pushed firmly into the ground so that each decoy is level with the ground. The decoy flock should have four feeders to each goose with a "sentinel head." The larger percentage of feeders looks more natural to decoying birds.

Geese always feed on the highest ridges so as to have better vantage. A large flock of decoys always has a couple of sentinels stationed slightly higher than the feeding flock. The decoy sentinels should also be placed in this manner.

If you're using all silhouettes for decoys, some of them should be "quartered," turned at angles, heads turned partially into the wind. Thus the decoying birds will still see some profiles as they "wheel" toward the decoys. Good pits, good decoys and good calling will produce good goose shooting.

Shooting Feeding Geese in Other Areas

Sagebrush

Few people know it but geese like to eat the cheetgrass found in the sagebrush areas of the Western U.S. and Canada. They eat the tender green shoots found in late fall. The green cheetgrass only occurs in years that we have fall rains.

The geese love this grass and will fly miles to get it. Shooting geese in cheetgrass is kind of a day-to-day thing and when you spot geese feeding in it you should shoot there that day or the next morning.

Geese are wary about feeding near tall sagebrush and will stick to little open flats. The best way to conceal yourself is to find a little swale, dig a pit and drape yourself with green undertaker cloth or some camouflage cloth. Put lots of decoys out in the same manner we discussed in field shooting and you're in business.

Irrigated Pastures

A goose is as fond of irrigated pasture as domestic livestock is. When you find them feeding in places like this, it calls for another pit operation. The cover to the pit should be covered with grass, then wire the grass on. Down through the years we have had good shooting in pastures. Simply follow the methods we have outlined in other types of field shooting.

COURTESY OF EDDIE BAUER

Flooded Grain Fields

In Chapter 18, we suggest flooding grainfields. This will produce some super shooting on both ducks and geese. The pits must however be waterproofed. Both the tank blind and Smitty's duck blind, as described in Chapter 2, work well under these conditions. You need a blend of both field decoys and floating decoys to have an effective setup. A few mallard decoys help set the stage.

Pass Shooting

Pass shooting is best practiced next to game refuges or some other area that is a natural holding area for geese. The birds can be shot as they pass to and from these areas. Your effectiveness will be determined mostly by the weather. Fog and wind are most helpful as both conditions will make the birds fly much lower. Bluebird weather is absolutely the poorest time to consider pass shooting. If you're pass shooting an area adjacent to a waterfowl refuge, your success in part will be determined by the amount of other hunters in the area. If they're all scratch shooting, you're not going to have a very high success ratio.

Potential Pass Shooting Areas

I'd stay away from federal and state waterfowl refuges except under exceptional weather conditions — fog, wind and snow. Under these conditions you'll get some birds. Spend your time looking for secluded lakes geese fly in and out of. Look for marshes the geese fly into off tidal flats. They like the aquatic growth found in the marsh and you can have a crack at them as they come and go.

You can get some good pass shooting adjacent to fields the geese are feeding in. Don't shoot at the first couple of flocks that go into the field. Instead, let them act as decoys. The subsequent flocks will drop lower and lower and your chances of success will be vastly improved.

A final note on pass shooting. Pass shooting is like the lyrics from "September Song" — "A waiting game."

Caution on Pass Shooting

Don't pass shoot your own water area. This will have a traumatic effect on the birds using the area. You're better off to bide your time and just shoot your area with a decoy operation.

Goose Hunting Digest

Never move when geese are decoying. They can detect the slightest movement. Geese have monocular vision because their eyes are located on each side of the head. The bird, therefore, moves its head to establish a vision field.

Don't call when geese are directly overhead. Geese have sharp hearing and are extra-sensitive to high-pitched sounds. They can pinpoint where the calls are coming from. Let the geese "wheel," then resume calling.

Avoid shooting at large flocks of geese if you can get your limit from small ones. It's better to scare five than five hundred.

Remember, geese are bigger birds than ducks and it's very easy to deceive yourself into believing that they're closer than they actually are. When birds are decoying, most hunters waste lots of good effort by firing *too soon*.

A good guide is to wait until you can see a Canada's white cheek patch very distinctly. When you can see the patch clearly, the birds are *getting* in range. The bead or gun sight should cover the bulk of the goose. A decoying goose, at forty yards or more, is almost impossible to kill.

To test the veracity of this statement, next time you shoot a goose, unload your gun and have your hunting partner pace off various reasonable yardages. Using the rib or bead of your shotgun as an estimator, have your partner hold up the goose, wings outstretched. Aim at the bird and make a mental note as to the percentage of the bird covered by the rib or bead. This calculation makes an excellent future reference as to whether a goose is in range or not.

Camouflaged Pit Blind. Pit is actually large enough for two shooters to fit comfortably. Decoys placed to left of pit, some in water and some stake-outs.

Properly arranged goose decoys. Pillbox blind is concealed on sandbar.

Full-bodied goose decoys in pasture grass.
Courtesy Herter's Inc.
Waseca, Minnesota

6' Screendoor, cover
with wired on stubble

STUBBLEFIELD PIT

Geese decoying into Eastern Washington stubble field.

Pass shooting. These geese are passing just in range over high cliff.
Courtesy George Leonard Herter

Hundreds of hungry geese coming in to our decoys. Note ones with cupped
wings are just ready to sit in.

Chapter II
BRANT AND
BRANT HUNTING

There are two species of Brant — American Brant and Black Brant.

The American Brant

The American Brant are strictly natives of the Atlantic Coast. They breed in the Arctic and winter as far south as Delaware. Their migration starts in late August or early September. By mid-November they are all on their winter grounds. American Brant differ from their Pacific cousin, the Black Brant, in that they are lighter colored.

The American Brant is small, slightly larger than a Canvasback or Mallard. He is a member of the goose family and bears some of his cousins' characteristics. He has a black head and a short neck. The neck has a white collar similar to the Canada Goose but the white patch is broken by small lines of black feathers. His back is grey-brown. The breast is black in the forepart turning whitish into the belly and tail.

In breeding, the American Brant usually has four to eight young each year. The youngsters can swim immediately upon being exposed to the water. In migration, its long wings allow it to make good time.

American Brant Hunting

Because of its limited range, very few hunters get much exposure to them. Being a coastal bird, they do not get inland. There are several ways to hunt them however.

They only come in shore to feed, so you either have to get them while they're feeding, sneak them while they're rafted up offshore, or pass shoot them.

Decoying Brant

Brant, for the most part, feed on eelgrass. As eelgrass is available only on low or slack tides, shooting is dependent on the tide rather than shooting hours.

The idea is to locate your blind near where the birds are feeding, on a spit, a peninsula or a group of rocks.

If you find a good spit near some eelgrass beds, dig your pit. The birds will fly across the spit in going from one feed bed to another. As brant decoy well, particularly near feeding grounds, you can get your share by putting out a good "stool." Two hundred decoys is not uncommon.

If you find some rocks that are exposed at low tide, make a right-angle wire frame and cover it with kelp. Then place the decoys around the rocks. You can then sit up against the rocks with one of the wire frames in the water and the other portion acts as a roof.

Old-time brant decoys were carved from wood and some of them are still in use. L.L. Bean has an excellent Brant decoy available. The decoy is made from cork and as you can see is very lifelike.

Sneaking Brant

As Brant raft up in bays, river deltas and tidal flats, you can sometimes get them by sneaking them. A well-camouflaged boat or a scull boat will do it. You'd better check your state regulations on the use of scull boats. Scull boats are very effective and will enable you to "scull" right into a Brant flock.

Pass Shooting Brant

There are two methods of pass shooting Brant. One is to regularly watch the birds until you find a point of land or other spot that they regularly pass over in feeding. If you find such a spot, you're in good shape as Brant never fly very high except in migration.

The second method again calls for regularly watching the birds. When you know for sure where they're rafted up, wait for a foggy day and then anchor just short of the "raft" and shoot the birds as they come in shore to feed.

Brant Calling

Brant are one of the few birds that can be called orally — that is without any mechanical device. If you can imitate their principal sounds, you can call them right in. Their principal sounds are "Car-r-rup, R-r-rouk" and "Chronk, Chronk." They respond most readily to their babble "Kata-kata." This call I cover in the section on Black Brant.

The Black Brant

The Black Brant is very similar to the American Brant but can be distinguished from his eastern cousin by his considerably duskier appearance. His breast and undercarriage are much darker than the American Brant.

In productivity, Black Brant have three to eight youngsters each year. The Black Brant sticks to the Pacific Coast. It breeds primarily in Alaska and Siberia. It has a split winter range in that some flocks follow a route which takes them to Japan to winter while other flocks winter on the North American side — British Columbia to California.

There is always lamenting on the Pacific Coast by British Columbia, Washington, Oregon and California gunners that Brant season should be in the spring rather than the fall. Here on the West Coast we see most of our Brant in February, March and April. The State of Washington Game Department takes some pity on Washington Brant hunters and runs the season into February.

Black Brant Hunting

Black Brant shooting is, of course, very similar to American Brant hunting. The birds have basically the same habits so the methods we have related for American Brant will work as well; namely, decoying Brant, sneaking Brant and pass shooting Brant.

The following is, however, another method not practiced to any extent on the East Coast but in wide use on the West Coast.

The Piling Method of Taking Brant

The Black Brant's love for eelgrass is his downfall and the West Coast shooter takes advantage of this weakness. There are lots of professional pile drivers who go around making their living by driving piling for docks, piers, etc. Long ago some ingenious Brant hunter figured, "If the Brant won't come close to me, I'll get out with the Brant." He then picked a bay or tideflat that had lots of eelgrass, hired a pile driver, went into the bay and drove some piling. A small box is fixed to the top of the piling and the shooters sit in this. A huge stool of decoys, at least 100, is placed near the box.

The Brant will come on ebb tide near low slack to feed on eelgrass. This is a most successful method! Some of these piling blinds are located as much as three-quarters of a mile offshore. The trick is to have somebody run you out by boat — a guide or a friend. They then wait several hundred yards away and pick up the downed birds. The best setups are owned by private individuals who supply decoys, blinds and the boat all for about $25 per gun which is quite reasonable.

The Babble Call for Brant

As I mentioned earlier, Brant will respond quite well to an oral call. This is called the babble call. The rest of their calling is very similar to the American Brant.

The babble call is accomplished by imitating the sound "Ka-ta, Ka-ta, Ka-ta." This is repeated approximately ten times. It must be done with intermittent clicking of the tongue.

Both species of Brant test the taste buds as the eelgrass they feed on produces an excellent flavor.

I recently talked to an old Washington Coast "Salt" about Brant hunting and after a rather lengthy oration from him, I asked if he had anything else to say about Brant shooting. He said, "Yes, it's colder than hell out there!"

Salt water Brant decoy.
Courtesy L. L. Bean, Inc.
Freeport, Maine

Chapter 12
THE ART OF JUMP SHOOTING

Jump shooting is like playing Baccarat. The element of surprise is always there. Unlike shooting decoying birds, or pass shooting, there is no get-ready time. The speed of human reaction in the normal individual has been calculated at a quarter of a second. A bird will respond faster than that but you can put yourself on equal terms with the birds in several ways.

Always assume the bird is there. If you practice this rule you're going to be ready when the bird isn't, and that's the trick. As you approach each bend of a stream, approach it with conviction. Say to yourself, "There's a bird here and I'm going to get him!"

Use the weather to your advantage, particularly the wind. All birds operate on the principle of aerodynamics. If you remember this you'll get more birds. When jump shooting a stream, walk into the wind. If you're walking into the wind and a bird jumps up, the bird will be hampered and slowed down by the wind. This, of course, works to your advantage. If you walk with the wind the bird has the advantage because once he's launched himself, he sails and in no time at all he's gone.

The third factor in jump shooting is bird control. If you can make the birds fly and fly where you want them to, you have it made. This might sound difficult but it's really not. If we assume the birds are there, use the weather to our advantage, and control the birds, we're ready to begin "organized jump shooting."

Organized Jump Shooting

If we are to get our share of birds we need binoculars, rubber boots, sunglasses, a good retriever and a partner. The binoculars we'll use to "spot" birds on creeks, potholes and lakes. The rubber boots or waders will keep our feet dry and give us a little more flexibility as to where we can walk. Sunglasses come in handy if we're looking into the sun. When a bird jumps up, always try to have the advantage on the bird.

With a "good retriever" you can recover the birds you shoot. I say "good retriever" because a bad one is a liability. The dog should "heel" until the bird is shot. If he ranges too far, he's going to flush birds out of range. If the dog "heels" well and holds in close, you'll get lots of birds. If he doesn't meet both these qualifications, leave him in the car.

Your partner or partners are the "topping" on your shooting success. With a good partner you'll get appreciably more birds because of your ability to control the birds. One person can't control the birds but two can. Partners in jump shooting are as important as any other participation sport. Get a good one!

Bird Control in Jump Shooting

Potholes

In the illustration "Pothole Jump Shooting" we have a small pothole surrounded on three sides by high cliffs. The south end of the pothole is open, the terrain at the south end is a fairly flat, sagebrush draw. The trick here is to get the birds to fly out the north end toward the two "shooters". This is accomplished by the "stalker" going around to the south end of the pothole and making his way through the cover. The "stalker" then gives a loud war whoop which flushes the birds.

As the "stalker" is covering the only good exit, the birds are forced to fly out over the cliffs. It's the natural inclination of all creatures to go in the opposite direction of sound particularly when they are startled. The birds in this particular situation will go due north and over the plateau where we have the "shooters" waiting. You will note in the illustration that we have a "shooter" stationed on each side of the plateau. This gives us good coverage, as the birds may pull more to one side than the other. If the birds do favor one side it will compensate itself when the shooter on that side fires — the birds will flare over the other shooter. The ideal situation, of course, is to have the birds go right up the middle — then we have real "bird control."

Lakes

Jump shooting lakes is generally a little more difficult. Large lakes are usually quite flat around the shorelines which makes for hard work when it comes to jump shooting them. However, most lakes have a sheltered bay or two. When the wind is gusty the birds will raft up in the bays. The birds will normally favor the lee side of the bay which is the side most sheltered from the wind. Some birds will sit in the water, while others will sit on the bank unless the shoreline is too abrupt.

The best way to spot exactly where the birds are is to pick a good vantage point and "glass" the bay with your binoculars. Once you've pinpointed the birds, start your approach route. You should pick your route carefully using whatever cover is around. Avoid ridges and stick to the draws. There's less chance of being spotted by the birds that way.

The very thing that creates a sheltered bay will now serve to your advantage. In the illustration shown here, "Jump Shooting a Lake," a high bluff shelters the bay the birds are in. The wind is blowing stiffly from the south which is creating a good "chop" on the lake. All we have to do here is proceed through the cover to the edge of the bluff. In walking avoid going through anything that will create noise. Walk ten or fifteen yards, then stop for a couple of minutes. This way, if you have made some noise, it gives the birds an opportunity to settle down. You and your partner should be at least several yards apart because the birds may have moved slightly and by separating you improve your odds on being close enough to the birds to shoot.

The illustration shows the wind blowing from the south. It could, of course, be blowing from any direction which would create different conditions. It's a good idea to take a walk around different lakes making mental notes as to the bays and good jump shooting routes. This will help you get birds later.

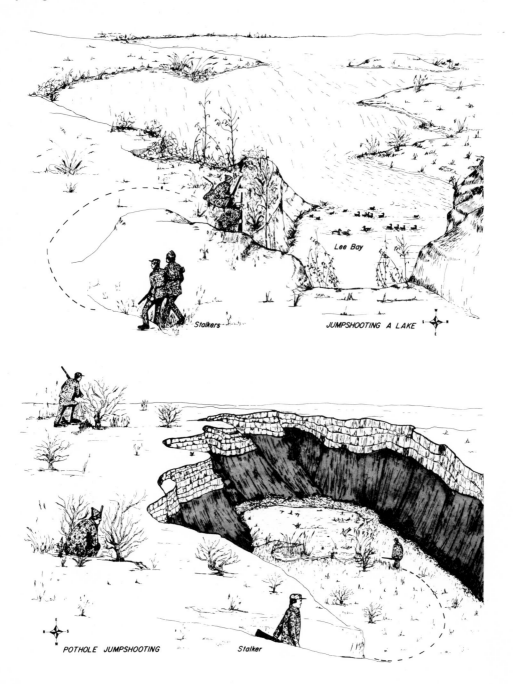

Lee Bay

Stalkers

JUMPSHOOTING A LAKE

POTHOLE JUMPSHOOTING

Stalker

Creeks

Jump shooting creeks has now become a sophisticated science. People used to blunder pell-mell through the brush along the water area and never had any particular "game plan." If a duck jumped up they shot it.

The correct method entails taking a given section of creek and covering it rather methodically. If there is no wind at all, the most profitable way is to drive your partner to one end of the creek area you're going to hunt. Then drive back to the opposite end yourself. Both of you should have binoculars so that you can "glass" each straight stretch and spot the birds.

In the illustration "Jump Shooting a Creek" the shooter stands on a knoll and with his binoculars checks as much creek as he can from his vantage point. When you spot the birds, pull back from the stream's edge so that you don't expose yourself. Then make a detour to the place exactly parallel to where you spotted the birds. Then walk up and flush them.

The need for having your partner coming from the opposite direction is twofold. First, he may flush birds over you that got up out of range as he approached them. Second, he should be on the opposite bank from you so that you can pick up each other's birds as some of them are bound to fall on the opposite bank. This is particularly important if the stream is deep and swift which is hard on your dog.

The Summary of Jump Shooting

Jump shooting is a fun phase of duck hunting. It's exciting and good exercise as it involves much more walking than other forms of duck hunting. With the ever present surprise element I look forward to bends in the creek or to what lies around the next knoll.

To be successful at jump shooting requires careful planning. You should study terrain and contour maps. In the summer go through the area you plan to jump shoot the coming fall and look at the approaches to each pothole and lake. Dry run a walk along the creeks, know each bend well. If you do all these things, it'll pay off for you!

Knoll

"Jump Shooting a Creek"

Glassing a creek. The idea here is to spot the birds and plan your attack.

Jumping them up.

Chapter 13
WATCHING, WEATHER AND WATERFOWL

Ever watch a flight of ducks appear on the horizon and then suddenly disappear in the opposite direction? If you stick around and watch, in a few moments another flock of ducks will appear and render exactly the same performance. Ducks are distinct creatures of habit and if you take the time and patience to observe what they do, your success in hunting them will be increased by 300 percent.

The most motivating factor for a duck is weather. He migrates, unlike his cousin the goose, not by instinct but by weather. If you notice a sharp drop in temperature in your area or you anticipate that freezing and icing conditions will prevail, it is senseless to go to your favorite pothole because, very simply, the birds will not be there. Look for running water (creeks, brooks, rivers) or deep water. Deep water will not freeze in extremely cold conditions as long as there is wind. These are all excellent places to look for birds when cold weather is evident.

The greedy Mallards we find here in the Western States will sit on a frozen lake long after a truck could be driven on the ice as long as he can get one commodity — food. He will fly to get a drink of water but will stay right where he is as long as there is plenty of food.

Have you ever been on a lake with your decoys out in front of the blind and noticed that flock after flock of ducks are all lighting in the same place and not where you are shooting? The reason for this is the wind. Mr. Mallard does not like to get his feathers ruffled so consequently he seeks a lee bay or sheltered shoreline. In building blinds you should, on a given body of water, locate them so that they are all-purpose and all-weather. You should build several blinds so that regardless of the weather you are in a position to shoot. It is obviously a lot of work to build a great many blinds; however, the number of birds you shoot will be directly proportional to the effort you expend.

You can establish where you put the blinds in a rather simple manner by merely watching the birds. If you have absolutely no wind and the lake has a pronounced point of land or points of land, a blind or blinds should be located there. If you have a north wind, that is a wind blowing from the north, the birds will seek out a lee bay to the south that protects them from the wind. Under these conditions the blind should be located in the lee bay. The converse of this would be that if the wind were blowing from the south, the birds would light to the north in the lee bay that affords them shelter from the south wind. The same application would also be true for lakes lying east and west or wind blowing from east to west and vice versa. You may at this time refer back to Chapter 3, where the pictures illustrate the proper location of blinds under the wind conditions mentioned.

Both wind and snow will seriously affect the feeding habits of ducks and geese. In goose hunting, for example, suppose you have spotted a field in which geese have been feeding and you plan to hunt it the next morning. During the night a stiff wind comes up and is blowing from the opposite direction from the body of water the geese are using. The geese will not fight their way against the wind. This is particularly true in wheat fields and rice fields in the Western United States where the birds will sometimes journey fifteen to twenty miles to feed. Instead, the birds will stay close to the reserve or lake they are using even though it affords less feed.

A good bet under these conditions is to have access to a backup field close to the reserve. Birds quickly get a field cleaned up but sometimes, because of the wind, will go back to that same field they have fed in earlier in the season. You may already have pits in such a field. When it comes to the wind and a goose's feeding habits, the man who coined the phrase, "A wild goose chase" was not too far from wrong.

Ducks will move from large bodies of water as soon as the wind picks up if there are no sheltered bays. When they leave they head straight for water that offers them shelter from the wind. Good places to look are potholes that lie in canyons or draws. Brushy creeks are good. They'll even go to another large lake if part of it is sheltered.

If a person can fit part of his hunting around weather it will increase his success quite sharply. If the weather is real bluebird, the birds will only fly for the first hour in the morning; then they will raft up on the lake. Sometimes on days like this you're ahead to go to work. If your job will allow it, work when the weather is good and knock off when it changes to good hunting weather. My office sits about a half mile from a large lake, but high enough to afford me a look at the lake. I have a pair of binoculars in my office and if the wind gets a little gusty I start watching bird activity. If the air traffic gets heavy I head for a sheltered pothole and throw a few decoys out. If it's late in the afternoon I head for the corn or wheat fields as the wind will send birds out to feed a little earlier than usual.

When the first snowfall comes, ducks for some mysterious reason head for running water. If it's snowing when you go to bed at night, try shooting running water in the morning rather than lakes or potholes. Ducks seem to have a fetish about it and will head straight for creeks, brooks and rivers after they finish feeding. Of course, if you don't have access to running water you'll have to stick to your normal shooting areas.

If you have a significant temperature drop to the zero range, ducks will feed twice per day, morning and night, rather than their normal habit of feeding all night. This is applicable in areas where there are lots of grainfields. Geese normally feed morning and night anyway but will spend more time at it in zero weather. If snow should occur during zero weather both ducks and geese will feed all day.

The reasons for their increased feeding habits are rather basic. They need more food to produce body heat when the temperature drops and are also anticipating migrating and know they will need more food energy to make the trip. You can capitalize on their requirements by spotting the fields they're using and setting up decoys and blinds or pits.

Geese are great creatures of habit. They're also pretty good navigators. I've spent hundreds of hours watching geese particularly in relation to the manner in which they leave lakes I hunt them on. If you spend a few mornings or evenings watching them leave to go out to feed, you'll note that they have regular routes just like airlines. The reason for this is that they utilize air currents. A goose, knows that the shortest distance between two points is a straight line. Being smarter than most of us, he takes the line of least resistance.

Several things can put Mr. Honker in the roasting pan. In your observations of his "route" you'll note that if the wind was minimal he passed by the same places, attained about the same altitudes, and flew at approximately the same speed. If you can locate the exact places he flys over, he'll be in shooting range under several conditions: when he's not been molested such as on opening day, when it's foggy he flies lower than his normal altitude, and when it's windy he'll get right down on the "deck" to go out to feed. If you invest a few hours in watching where he goes out to feed you'll quickly spot a place that you'll have a good shot at him.

Everybody is always waiting for the "Northerns" to show up. Sometimes, however, we miss them. There are a couple safeguards against this: newspapers and radios. As most of our birds originate in the Canadian Provinces, a daily look at the temperatures there is a pretty good indication as to when the birds will come. If the temperature at night is 28° or warmer it won't push many birds out; however, when it gets 10° to 20° lots of birds will move. At less than 10° there will be a wholesale migration. If you have a short-wave radio or can pick up some Canadian stations you can predict this more specifically.

Vacations and time off should be planned around the most favorable hunting conditions. Your local weather conditions should also be part of your hunting plans.

Aeration of Duck Ponds

In recent years modern manufacturing developments allow us to keep our duck ponds open even in zero temperatures. This is accomplished through aeration of the surface water.

Aeration simply means causing water to circulate. Circulation is effected by using a floating pump, a few short lengths of pipe and a power source. The cheapest source is electricity but gasoline-operated pumps work just as well though not quite as economically. Electric pumps are equipped with a safety device so that if the power fails the pumping unit will not be damaged.

With the use of aeration you can keep your duck ponds open when everyone elses' ponds are frozen up. Costs of the pumps vary from $110 to $275 but are worth it if you have a source of cheap power nearby.

Chapter 14
RETRIEVING AND RETRIEVERS

Retrieving is a subject that will never be covered in one book much less one chapter. We will attempt to cover the most important aspects of retrieving and retrievers as they pertain to waterfowl shooting. Training has its rewards and its frustrations. Under today's hunting conditions, it's a most important factor. Fewer birds need be shot and more birds will be taken home by using a good retriever than will ever be taken home without one.

There are three basic reasons for using a retirever. The first, of course, is to conserve game. Statistically only 50 percent of all birds hit are killing shots. It then becomes mandatory that we conserve waterfowl as one of our most valuable resources. We have the satisfaction of knowing that we've conserved a bird that might otherwise have been lost.

The second reason for using retrievers is the wonderful companions they make. Most dogs are far more loyal than most humans. A dog's love for his master can be so pronounced that he may even follow his master to a sure death at the same time his natural instincts tell him that danger lurks.

The third reason for using retrievers is the satisfaction derived from watching the dog doing what he's been trained to do. The dog loves to please. He also loves to be praised for it.

Section 1 - The Dog

The dog is far more important than the breed. If the dog has the *good*, basic characteristics that can be molded into a good retriever, then that's the dog we're looking for even if it's a poodle!

There are several things to look for in selecting your dog:

1. Natural Ability — Natural ability is the most important factor in picking a dog. The more natural instinct the dog has, the more easily he can be adapted to your specific desires. If we were to pick out a puppy from a litter of six-week-olds, we should determine the boldest one, the one who's outgoing.

There are a couple of tests to try on them. Put them on a lawn chair and one will cower in the back, one looks over the edge and cries a little and then goes back and sits down. Another looks over the edge and bails off — now that's the one I'm interested in! Show them a pigeon. Look for their reaction. Take into account this is something they've never seen. You'll see some dogs actually afraid of a pigeon. That doesn't mean they can't be trained to like the pigeon; but the more aggressive ones will regard the bird as a challenge and be curious enough to get close to the bird. If you have a choice, take the aggressive one. These are just a few insights to natural ability.

2. Temperament and Personality — Each breed has given characteristics and given traits. It's very important to match the dog's personality with the owner's. Dogs of different breeds vary in personality. Dogs within the same breed differ to some degree.

We would never recommend that a person who is an introvert, a quiet, easygoing person take on a Chesapeake. Nor would I recommend that an outgoing person who tends to be pushy end up with a Golden Retriever. Right off the bat there is a conflict of personality. It's important to match the personality of the dog with the master. If that can be done, a relationship can develop that will end up in a love for the animal by the owner and respect and love for the owner by the dog.

3. Environment and Adaptability — Nothing has as great an effect on a dog's personality as his environment. If a dog is used to being yelled at and "walked over," he will be withdrawn and temperamental when he grows up. By contrast, if he is used to minding and being part of the family, he'll be well behaved and well adjusted.

A young dog is like a small boy. If you told a child to bring you the newspaper and he said, "Drop dead!", he would have to be reprimanded! Sometimes he would need a swat. But after you have corrected the child, you wouldn't lock him in the bathroom and not speak to him for a week! Animals are no different. If the dog disobeys and you lock him in his pen and avoid him, he doesn't understand the treatment. If the dog disobeys, give him a swat. But when he performs, reach down and pat him on the head. He's part of the family so go on from here. The incident is forgotten and forgiven. This builds a relationship that lasts as long as the dog.

4. Male vs. Female — Each sex has some characteristics. Both can be trained to be good hunting dogs.

Females tend to be more "homebodied." Like little girls, they learn quicker than little boys. For the first two years, they'll generally do better than males. Females become more attached to the family. They're easier to train because they like to please and aren't as independent. Females come in heat twice a year. This is, of course, a problem if they come in heat during the hunting season. Recently pills have been developed that can change their fertility cycles so that they don't come in heat during hunting season. With a female you can sometimes recover your money by breeding her and selling the puppies.

If you are going to spay a female, she should be mature sexually, mature personality-wise and have had her training. A female needs all the aggressiveness she can get during her training.

Males tend to be more dominant and are a little harder to control. While they don't learn as quickly as females, they do learn well. Being larger and more rugged, they don't give up as quickly, particularly in rough going like high tides or heavy cover. Good males are in demand for "stud service." Males, of course, can be "hunted" anytime. Males will wander if allowed to; females tend to stay at home.

In summary, if you want a good homebody that's easy on shrubs, then a female is fine, particularly with the availability of the pill to alter her fertility cycle. On the other hand, if you want a tough, rugged animal that can retrieve under the worst conditions, then the male is the one for the job.

113

COURTESY OF EDDIE BAUER

Section 2 - The Breed

The six principle breeds of retrievers are the Chesapeake Bay Retriever, the Golden Retriever, the Labrador Retriever, the Curly-coated Retriever, the Flat-coated Retriever, and the Irish Water Spaniel. Any of these dogs will do the job. Each breed has certain characteristics and certain traits. As we discussed earlier in Section 1 of this chapter, you should try to find a dog with the personality and temperament to suit you.

You should also pick a dog that can get the job done. By that we mean a dog that is suited to retrieve under the conditions it will be exposed to. For example, a Chesapeake is more at home in high seas, zero temperatures and heavy icing conditions while an Irish Water Spaniel likes to work in swamps, heavy cover and more moderate temperatures.

You should evaluate the conditions the dog will be working under and let this enter into the selection of the best dog for you. We are going to cover some basic characteristics of each of the six breeds in order to give you an insight as to their adaptability to your needs.

1. The Chesapeake Bay Retriever — The Chesapeake is probably the least handsome of the retrievers but is probably the most rugged! Not many things will stop him from making the retrieve. He takes high seas, extreme cold and long swims all in stride. The dog loves water and loves to get wet. Some retrievers "gently" enter the water. The Chesapeake plunges into the water. His heavy coat is comprised of a thick outer layer of "guard" hairs plus a dense, fur-like inner coat similar to an otter. The coat itself seems almost self-lubricating as it oils itself and prevents the dog from getting wet clear through.

The dog is known for his memory and has an almost automatic capacity to "mark" down dead and crippled birds. If he sees one that is crippled, he'll pass the dead birds up in favor of getting the cripple first. Not the most affectionate of retrievers, he has many other virtues that offset this.

The Golden Retriever — The Golden Retriever is a descendant of the Russian Tracker who was a much bigger animal. The Russian Tracker weighed very close to 100 pounds. Modern Golden Retrievers weigh about sixty pounds at maturity. He is not as aggressive as a Chesapeake or a Lab, but is very affectionate.

The Golden is very "birdy" and possesses an exceptional nose. An easy dog to discipline, he responds well to training. The dog is soft-mouthed and enjoys retrieving. The Golden is more at home in cold water than people think. We've used them in the Arctic with no trouble at all.

3. The Labrador Retriever — The Lab, as he is sometimes called today, is the most common of all retrievers. Their feelings are not as easily hurt as a Golden and they are not as dominant and strong-willed as a Chesapeake. A Lab is intelligent and has lots of desire. He has an excellent nose and is willing to learn. The dog is hardy and will stand up under almost any climatic condition.

Labs, at present, win about 90 percent of the competition. Most people will say this is because there are more Labradors. Why are there more Labradors? Because Labs fulfill more people's desires of what they're looking for in a dog. A Lab is easier to train and that's basically why there are more Labrador Retrievers.

4. *The Curly-coated Retriever* — The Curly-coated Retriever has never attained the popularity of the Chesapeake, the Golden or the Labrador yet he's an excellent retriever. He is an eager dog and has no reluctance to dive into cold water. Smaller than the rest of the retrievers, only twenty-four pounds at maturity, he's an exceptional swimmer and possesses some of the Chesapeake's memory qualities. Because of his smaller size, the dog is particularly good in brush and his keen nose makes him a good tracker.

5. *The Flat-coated Retriever* — The Flat-coated Retriever presents something of a paradox as far as the United States is concerned. The breed traces its ancestry back to two breeds that are indigenous to the North American Continent. Yet it is one of the least known species of purebred dogs in America.

They are the offshoot of crossing the Labrador with the St. John's Newfoundland. While the breed was introduced to the United States many years ago, it has never mustered sufficient supporters to have a specialty club. As a consequence, specimens of the Flat-coated Retriever are not plentiful, although they may be found scattered through the shooting country.

6. *The Irish Water Spaniel* — The Irish Water Spaniel was an early arrival in North America. He got a head start on both the Chesapeake and the Labrador.

The dog is the largest of the Spaniel family. The dog works well in both open country and brush. He's at home in swamps or tidal bays. The dog is excellent for jump shooting and will work heavy cover and flush out those tight-holding mallards.

The Irish Water Spaniel is a strong swimmer and can be started on retrieving lessons almost as soon as obedience. The dog runs to the temperamental side and requires lots of patience. Once trained, however, you've got a good retriever and companion for a long time.

Section 3 - The Training

Now that we've selected the dog and the breed, we come to the hard part, training. Training is a subject that people never seem to run out of words on. But, it all boils down to some basics and one *prime fact* — 90 percent of a good retriever is his willingness to *obey*. The most important thing in a dog's training is pure *obedience*. He must have a built-in response to each thing you ask of him. With this in mind we'll go through our format.

When to Get the Dog

You should get the dog when he is between five and eight weeks of age. He should be exposed to everything you can think of — birds, noise, people, riding, rules of the house, etc. In other words, treat him like a small child. You get him used to being around you. His future work should take the form of fun and now when he's a puppy you can build some good characteristics in him that will last him the rest of his life. Throw him a bumper or a duck wing have him bring it back then reward him with affection and praise.

Don't reward him with material things like cookies or someday you'll find yourself running out of cookies in the duck blind. The first few months around you are very important in getting him ready for his training days.

The Time to Start Training

Normally the best time to start formally training your dog is when he is about eight months old. By then he's learned some simple responses and he's developing his memory bank. You'll want to take into account that he remembers the good as well as the bad. Make everything just as pleasant as possible for him. Then you've gained his confidence.

Good Dog Psychology

Before you start to train a dog you should understand the four cardinal rules of good dog training. Briefly as possible, here they are.

1. Never Repeat Yourself! — The dog has to be made to understand that he has to mind the first time a command is given. If he doesn't respond immediately, he should be corrected. When you say sit, for example, and he doesn't sit down, then swat him right on the fanny. And when he sits down, just as quickly pat him on the head. In five minutes you'll have a dog that knows when you say sit that's exactly what he should do. He'll wag his tail and look for the pat.

2. Be Consistent! — Always use the same word and tone of voice and always correct a dog the first time he does not respond.

3. Don't Try to Control a Dog with Your Voice! — No yelling or hollering. The dog should mind or respond to a given stimulus no matter who says it, how it is said or when or where it is said. How would you like to have to yell at your dog to make him stay just as the geese were decoying?

4. You're Always the Boss! — A well-trained hunting dog never questions your authority. It is not enough for him to think you are boss, he has to know it! You may not always be right, but you are always boss!

Training School Begins

The Basic Commands

There are several basic commands: heel, sit, stay, down and come.

1. Heel — A dog that heels should walk quietly by your side without restraint with his head roughly equal with your knee. If you shoot right-handed, your dog should be on your left side. If you shoot left-handed, your dog should be on your right side. The important thing in heeling is that the dog is there at all times. He is not sniffing the ground; he's with you. The dog should be watching where you go. If you turn, the dog turns. You don't bump into the dog. You're not following the dog; he's following you.

To accomplish this initially, you use a 6-foot leash and only the word "heel." If he strays too far, restrain him with the leash; then tell him to "heel." He soon learns the command "heel" means stay by your side. With the leash and the command "heel" you can also regulate which side he's on.

2. *Sit* — When you want the dog to sit, say "sit"; then push him into position and pat him when he's there. Keep practicing this until the dog knows the command. There is no punishment, just discipline. His reward is the pat on the head. The important thing is that once the dog has learned the command, you should demand from him that he respond to the command at all times whether he wants to or not.

3. *Stay* — To make the dog steady he must sit and stay while the birds are being thrown during training and while they're being shot while hunting. This is accomplished by discipline. You can start by putting a choke collar and leash on him and having someone throw the birds. Then gently hold him in tow even if he wants to go. When he responds to the word "stay" take the collar off and again have someone throw the birds. Repeat this until the dog knows he can't go until you release him. With some dogs it may be necessary to give more physical pain than a choke collar and leash. You may have to use a slingshot or an electrified wire. But getting him disciplined will save you much misery when the birds are decoying. When he's thoroughly adjusted to the command "stay," we release him with the command "back" which we'll discuss later.

4. *Down* — Not the most important command but one that has merit. It's nice to have enough dog control that you can make him lie down when you want him to. Getting him to lie down has various practical applications — in motel rooms, in the blind, or when you're caught flat-footed outside the blind and birds are decoying. If you can get the dog to lie down his profile is automatically reduced. You can teach the dog to crawl up an irrigation ditch with you while you are trying to jump shoot some ducks. This is all accomplished with discipline. Ask him to lie down, forcing him gently with the flat of your hand. If he doesn't respond, try it again only a little more forcefully. Then if he doesn't lie down, give him a little swat. Be sure to go easy between each attempt. He'll come around.

5. *Come* — The command "come" is an important command and it's probably the one that most owners or trainers have the most trouble with. It's a frustrating command to teach because when you don't get the response you become irritated. After you've yelled "come" several times and the dog finally responds, you give him a swat or correction. As far as the dog is concerned the only reason he got the correction was for coming. This is just exactly the opposite of what you want. When the dog hears the command "come," he should want to come. He should also not be afraid to come to you.

How do you teach it? First, put him into a situation in which he cannot help but come. When you say "come," have him on a check cord or some other means of restraint, so that you physically cause him to come. At that point reward him for obeying the command. Continue this procedure until there is absolutely no doubt that when the command is given, he'll respond. Until this point, you've had him in a position where he did not have to make up his mind. Now take off the check cord. Put him in an enclosure which will make it easy for him to respond to the command. If he doesn't come, he must be corrected but not by you. You have to avoid the dog's realizing that you caused the correction. Then make him come to you. When he comes, praise him. It takes a lot of work but it must be instilled in the dog.

Release Commands

In the discussion of release commands we get into a very grey area. Some trainers release the dog for the retrieve by using the *dog's name*. The dog's name then becomes a release command. This is actually confusing to the dog because he then has to rely on the inflection in your voice to determine what's requested of him. You'll use his name many times, so will other people. The dog shouldn't have to judge the tone each time his name is spoken.

1. Fetch as a Release Command — We do use the word "fetch" in training, but normally it's a derogatory command. It's a command that means pick it up or else. Sooner or later the dog will run into something he doesn't want to pick up. Dogs in training for competition are "force broke." They retrieve not only because they want to but because they are told to.

A good dog has to be force broke because someday when the water is cold, he's going to retrieve because he's told to. To get that response, we use the command "fetch." Because the dog has had a lot of correction associated with the word "fetch," we don't like to use it as a release command.

2. Back, the Proper Release Command — We have discussed the disadvantages of using the dog's name and the dog's corrective association with the word "fetch." In some dogs, both the name and "fetch" will work as a release command but why put the dog at a disadvantage.

The same word should mean the same thing no matter who says it, where it is said or how it is said. We use the word "back." Professionally, in the last few years, more dogs have been released on the word "back" than any other command.

This is the reason we use "back": Later on when you give the dog the college course which goes into waterfowl training in depth, the dog must respond to hand signals. He ignores his eyes, his nose, his natural instincts and goes exactly where he's told by hand signals. We're now talking about a well-disciplined dog, one that's under control, who all his life has only left your side on the word "back."

The most difficult response to get from a dog is for the dog to go farther away from you when he has already gone out, say 150 yards or so. When you're teaching him hand signals, he sits out there and you blow your whistle and raise your hand and say "back." It becomes the easiest command because he's always left you on that word. You say "back" and he moves farther away. The dog will look to you for direction and with the whistle and the hand signals, you can direct him right to the bird. It's a simple command and one that gets the best results. Just keep him at your side until you're ready to release him.

Professional Training

Depending on your vocation, you may have lots of time or none. If you have lots of time, it's nice to spend it with your dog going through the basics. If you don't have the time, the dog is better off in the hands of a professional trainer.

A "pro" is probably going to produce a product that is more highly proficient in a shorter period of time. If you do have a pro work your dog, we'd like to emphasize the importance of working with the pro before taking your dog home.

The pro will first gain the dog's confidence and then begin the training. The dog is in a new environment and the pro becomes his master. Go out with the pro. Go through the paces. Handle the dog with the pro. Learn the commands. Shoot a few birds over him. Then take him home. When you get the dog home don't slack off. Keep the discipline and commands up. The dog will develop a new attitude and be happy.

To send a dog to a trainer and never work him while he's there would be a mistake. You're not going to know the commands or how to cope with the dog's mistakes.

Cost of Professional Training

Normally an obedience course which lasts about a month costs $100. This takes the dog through all the basic commands and gets him ready for higher learning.

His training should be broken into several segments occurring about every ninety days. If you're bringing the dog along yourself, you probably can get by until just before hunting season, then the dog should have a refresher course.

The College Course

After the dog has hunted for a year, he should go back to the trainer for a little college training. This course involves hand signals, behavior and some of the more sophisticated professional concepts. A course like this is quite expensive and will run about $250, which is a nominal price to pay for the finished product.

Books on Retrieving

There are a number of fine books on training retrievers. It's a good idea to have one of them in your library. A couple of excellent ones are *Training Retrievers for Field Trials and Hunting* by Paul E. Shoemaker, Superior Publishing Company, Seattle, Washington; *Training Your Retrievers*, by James Lamb Free; *Waterdog*, by Richard A. Wolters; and *Charles Morgan on Retrievers*.

Chapter 15
GUNS, AMMUNITION AND SHOOTING TECHNIQUES

In the preceding chapters we have discussed many of the things that are essential for successful waterfowl shooting. Good blinds, decoys, calling and habitat are all basic necessities for good shooting. Each of them are like supporting actors in a well-executed play. They all perform their parts and now you alone are left on stage to end the play.

The birds have responded to your call and begin their last "wheel" over the decoys. With one fluid motion you rise, swing with the bird and fire. If you executed your movements smoothly, you should have gotten the bird. If you missed, some factor in your shooting motion was out of order and must be corrected. Before we get into the subject of corrective techniques, we should first discuss two items --- the gun and the shells

The Gun

People have been using shotguns for decades and you might say shotguns have been using people. Shotguns don't hit birds, people do! A classic example of this was a situation that happened many years ago. I had stationed several "shooters" on a cliff north of a lake geese had been using. I told them the geese would lift off shortly after dawn to go out to feed. Each shooter was well concealed and about thirty-five yards from the edge of the lake.

At about twenty minutes after dawn the birds lifted off and headed straight for the shooters. It was a nice respectable flock of about 300 geese and the birds were well spread out. All seven shooters had a crack at some portion of the flock. Six of the shooters drew blanks, but the seventh, a little old man of about seventy, had gotten a double with his .28GA. The other six shooters had nothing to show for their efforts despite the fact they were shooting expensive modern shotguns of various makes and gauges. My point is the the little old man, not the gun, got the double!

Good guns are wonderful if they're properly used. If you don't know the capabilities of your gun, you will be handicapped in every calculation you make. Most modern-day shotguns will, at ranges such as thirty yards, be off their aiming center between six and eighteen inches. This, of course, has to be taken into account when firing at birds.

Statistically, 90 percent of all waterfowl will be killed at forty yards or less. This means the killing pattern of your gun should fall into that range. Shotgun manufacturers figure that a half dozen pellets will kill a bird at fifty yards if you're using a full-choked gun and 2 3/4-inch magnum shells. The average shooter is not that deadly at fifty yards, because a full-choked gun, regardless of gauge, will put slightly more than 50 percent of its charge into a 30-inch circle. A modified barreled gun will accomplish the same thing at forty-five yards, as will improved cylindered guns at thirty-five yards.

The gun, therefore, is merely a device for satisfying the shooter's desire to get the bird. When we consider that the bulk of all ducks and geese are shot at forty yards or less, then you should be shooting a gun that patterns best at those ranges.

You can accomplish this in a variety of ways. In the case of double barrels you can get combinations of modified and full barrels or improved cylinder and modified barrels. You'll get a little more flexibility with shorter barreled guns, either 26-inch or 28-inch rather tha 30-inch.

In using automatics or pumps, you're a bit more locked in because the gun will be bored to only one choke. Usually a 28-inch barrel bored modified is the most popular. However, in recent years, 26-inch improved cylinder guns are getting pretty common. For the shooter who likes to still take the "long" full-choke shot, he can stay flexible by having a Poly Choke or some other compensator installed on his gun. With the aid of a Poly Choke or compensator, you can adjust to the condition you are shooting under. When birds are decoying well, modified or improved cylinder works well. For badly flaring birds or pass shooting, you can change to full-choke. For ducks and geese, I personally wouldn't have an automatic or pump gun that didn't have an adjustable choke on it. The Poly Choke or some of the other compensators give you the flexibility of having five guns in one. Later in this chapter we'll discuss the adaptability of shotguns to the proper shooting techniques.

Waterfowl Guns

On the following pages we have pictured several excellent waterfowl guns. All of these guns are available in various barrel lengths. Each manufacturer has a wide choice of chokes as well as several different gauges. As most of the manufacturers offer catalogs, we suggest that you write them directly to get more specific information for your own use.

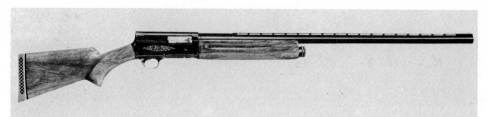

The Browning Automatic-5 12-gauge 3" magnum. Magnum also available in regular 12-gauge model. Courtesy Browning Arms Company, Morgan, Utah, 84050.

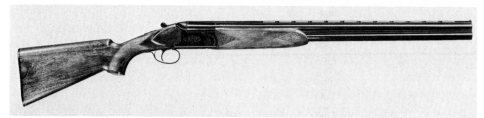

Courtesy Savage Arms, Westfield, Massachusetts, 01085

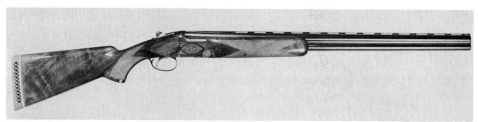

The Browning Superposed 12-gauge 3" magnum. Courtesy Browning Arms Company, Morgan, Utah, 84050

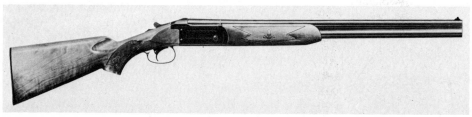

Courtesy Savage Arms, Westfield, Massachusetts, 01085

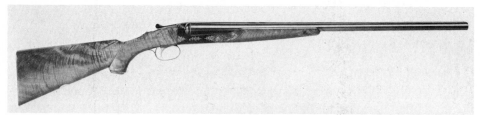

The Winchester Model 21, 12-gauge double. Courtesy Winchester-Western, New Haven, Connecticut, 06504

Harrington and Richardson Model 440, pump action, 12-gauge. Courtesy Harrington & Richardson Firearms, Worcester, Massachusetts, 01610

The Winchester Model 12 Super Pigeon. Courtesy Winchester-Western, New Haven, Connecticut, 06504

Courtesy Remington Arms Company, Bridgeport, Connecticut, 06602

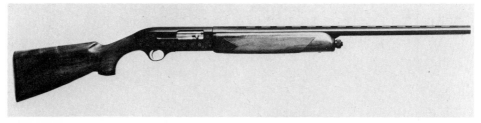

The Garcia-Beretta AL-2, 12-gauge automatic. Courtesy The Garcia Corp., Teaneck, New Jersey, 07666

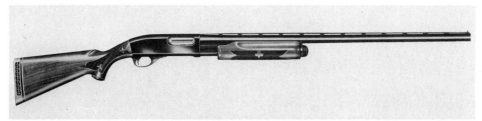

Courtesy Remington Arms Company, Bridgeport, Connecticut, 06602

Shotgun Shells and Shot

Shotgun shells and shot play an important part in your shooting success. There are many mistakes that can be made about shotgun shells one of which is trying to save money. We find people who drive hundreds of miles, stay in the best motels, hire guides, shoot a $600 shotgun and show up in the duck blind with a couple boxes of low-base shells, usually 7 1/2's. They saved $1.00 a box by buying low-base shells instead of high-base loads. They get less ducks in hand, cripple birds unnecessarily and have more gun malfunctions than they care to talk about. Shotgun shells are an area you shouldn't attempt to save a few pennies on. Go out to hunt with the best gun you can afford and use the best ammunition.

The size of the shot is an important item. Your shot pattern will vary because of the shooting range and it will also vary because of the shot size. Large shot pellets have a higher velocity at longer ranges and will also shoot a tighter pattern. Shotgun shell sizes refer to the size of the pellets in the shell. A shell containing #4 shot has less pellets than a shell containing #6 shot because the #4 shot is larger than the #6. The same amount of powder is pushing both loads. With the larger amount of pellets in the air, it would be logical to think you'd have a better chance of hitting the bird. In theory this is true; in application it is not because with smaller shot as distance increases velocity drops. The load is very important in relationship to the type of shooting. We have printed a chart to assist you in picking the load for the condition. The chart covers 12-, 16- and 20-gauge guns as well as 3-inch chambered 12-gauge. It does not cover .410- or 10-gauge shotguns.

Shell Casings

In recent years we have seen some rather startling changes in shell casings themselves — from the old brass base paper shot shells to the present brass base plastic shot shells which are made from polyethylene plastic.

The old paper shot shells used to fall apart and peel once they got wet. By contrast the modern plastic shell can be dropped in the water with no resulting problems.

The early plastic shells had some defects as the pellets could bulge out the shot shell case and cause varied and sometimes dangerous powder pressures. In some instances, you could actually feel the pellets through the shell case. Practices like these and violations of use of acceptable shell case material, along with shotguns themselves, come under the close scrutiny of an agency called SAAMI, Sporting Arms and Ammunition Manufacturers Institute. This group checks both shotguns and ammunition to make sure both the gun and the shells meet its minimum standards.

The Shell of Tomorrow

What will the shell of tomorrow be like? No one knows yet for sure but several shotgun shell manufacturers who are ecologically-oriented are working toward a shell that will be biodegradable or self-destructing. To date, no one to my knowledge has come up with a plastic or any other material that structurally will withstand the discharge velocity upon firing and that you could later expect to self-destruct. If they can accomplish this, it would be wonderful to relieve the country of the millions of shells that are annually scattered about.

The All-plastic Shell

I recently had the opportunity to tour Herter's ammunition plant in Waseca, Minnesota. I was personally escorted by George Leonard Herter, famous sportsman and author, who gave me the "shooters" tour of the plant. George showed me two eye-openers — their all-plastic shell and their spin-off wad.

The Shell Case

The shell case is made completely from space cone plastic. There is no brass at all. Herter guarantees that each shell case can be reloaded a minimum of ten times and needs no resizing.

The Spin-off Wad

These spin-off wads hold the shot charge together until the wad column leaves the barrel then spin off automatically to the right leaving the shot charge in shape for a dense high-velocity pattern.

Left: Herter's all plastic shotgun shell with spin-off wad. Right: Herter's all plastic shotgun shell with conventional star crimp.

Herter's Spin-off Wad. Courtesy Herter's, Inc., Waseca, Minnesota, 56093

Shooting Techniques

We now come to the time for practically applying what we've learned. The results should be your getting more birds.

First, I'd recommend that you have your gun "fitted," if you haven't already done so. "Fitting" involves a competent gunsmith tailoring your gunstock to make you feel comfortable. It might involve cutting off part of the stock or adding a recoil pad that will build the stock out to the proper length. In any event, it's money well-spent to have a good gunsmith fit your gun. Feeling comfortable with a gun is bound to have an effect on the number of birds you'll get. The saving you'll realize by using less ammunition will more than offset the cost of having your gun fitted properly.

Actual Shooting Conditions

We are now sitting in a nice comfortable blind scanning the horizon for a bunch of ducks or geese. Our "tailored" shotgun beside us, we're ready for action. A flock of mallards approach well within gun range. We rise up and swing on a fat Greenhead. Bang! A miss! The bird turns and flares. Another miss! The bird straightens out and on the third shot finally crumples. The other seven birds in the flock had flown in and out of the decoys and were never bothered. Darn poor shooting!

Obviously we need to determine the proper way to shoot. Rather than make some great mystery diagnosis of proper wing shooting, we'll break it down into simple, understandable language.

Man's Earliest Computers

Modern man has come up with some very sophisticated computers but none will ever equal the brain, reflex system and eyes. Properly used, they can produce deadly shooting.

You must have total coordination to get good results. The eyes are the most important. They spot the birds and activate the brain. Like radar, the eyes track the bird. The brain activates the body. The eye makes the proper calculation in distance and time and relates it to the brain. You then pull the trigger. Properly executed, you'll get the bird.

A basketball game would be a good parallel. Bob Cousy was one of the best all-time set shot artists. In a basketball game, the eye computes the distance, decides the proper arc, and the brain discharges the shot. Bob Cousy was good because of his ability to combine vision with his brain and reflexes. You can make the same application to shooting birds.

The Arc Method of Shooting

All objects in flight have a pattern or trajectory. Arc shooting is practiced by all successful shooters. They might call it impulse shooting or instinct shooting or a variety of other things, but it all boils down to hitting an object in flight by automatic calculation. This is best accomplished by the arc method.

The whole concept of arc shooting is to establish a smooth method of shooting. Once the birds are sighted and you've picked your first bird, automation begins. If you are shooting decoying birds, they are slowing down which is a plus in your favor. To successfully arc shoot, start your aim and swing from behind the bird. This is the initial phase of the arc. Continue the swing of your gun slightly faster than the bird is moving. When the gun passes the bird, you should instantly fire. Don't slow your gun motion down and the natural arc of your swing will keep pace with the bird and you should hit it. The trick to successful arc shooting is to fire immediately after the gun has passed the bird. Do this without slowing your swing. Your brain, eyes and reflex system do the rest.

If you properly follow the arc system and swing with the bird, it doesn't matter if the bird changes direction because you can follow the bird down if it's going to light in the decoys or up if it flares. Just stay with it!

To get more than one bird out of a flock requires your taking a minimal amount of time on all shots, or the other birds will be gone too quickly. Once you've mastered the arc method of shooting you can get quite automated which is the secret to successful waterfowl shooting.

A Study in Arc Shooting with Visual Aids

They say one picture is worth a thousand words! With the aid of artist Hope Cameron and some very fine photographs we will, on the next few pages, show some practical applications of proper arc shooting.

In both the artist's illustrations and the photographs, the circles shown directly ahead of the birds indicate the point at which the arc of your gun has *just* passed the bird. It's at this point that you shoot. Remember that in each scene, the arc of the gun is started behind the bird. You swing through the bird and then fire. Do not slow down your swing! After getting your first bird, go on to the next.

Conclusion

In the shooting scenes you have just looked at, we have tried to duplicate as many actual shooting conditions as possible. As it's impossible to anticipate all of the various shots you're going to take, we can only suggest that you try to analyze each one you take and try to figure out why you hit or missed the bird.

Even though you may have formerly practiced shooting with varied leads, if you give it a fair trial, you'll get more birds in the long run with the arc-swing method that most professional shooters use.

PROPER SHOTGUN SHELL LOADS

Ducks	Condition	Range	Choke	Geese
NO. 6 2¾" MAGNUM	DECOYING BIRDS	15 – 25 YARDS	IMPROVED CYLINDER	NO. 4, 6 2¾" MAGNUM
NO. 4 2¾" MAGNUM	DECOYING BIRDS	25 – 40 YARDS	MODIFIED	NO. 4 2¾" MAGNUM
NO. 4 2¾" MAGNUM	WINDY, FLARING BIRDS	40 – 50 YARDS	FULL	NO. 2, 4 2¾" MAGNUM
NO. 6 2¾" MAGNUM	JUMP SHOOTING	20 – 45 YARDS	IMPROVED MODIFIED	NO. 4 2¾" MAGNUM
NO. 6, 7½ 2¾" MAGNUM	CORNFIELD SHOOTING	15 – 25 YARDS	IMPROVED CYLINDER	NO. 2, 4 2¾" MAGNUM
NO. 4 2¾" MAGNUM	PASS SHOOTING	40 – 50 YARDS	FULL	NO. 2 2¾" MAGNUM
NO. 4 3" MAGNUM	PASS SHOOTING	50 – 70 YARDS	FULL	NO. 2, B.B. 3" MAGNUM

In this scene we have picked the leader. Should you miss, you have a chance at the second goose because of his proximity to the first goose.

In this flock we picked the hen. If you miss her, there are two drakes close behind.

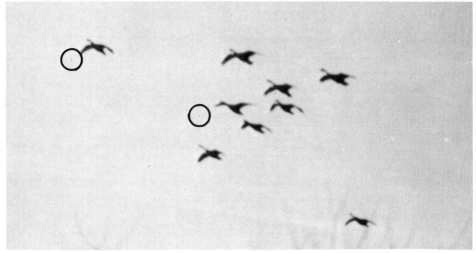

These geese are just setting down. You should be shooting slightly ahead and below them. Courtesy George Leonard Herter

Chapter 16
LOCATING A DESIRABLE SHOOTING AREA

If you are a longtime resident of the area you hunt, then your task of locating a good property is not as difficult as it would be for someone moving into the area and starting from scratch.

Resident or nonresident, it is my opinion that the best way to locate and evaluate hunting property is from the air. This is especially true if the area involved is a large one.

A study of maps of the region and a flight over it by plane can accomplish more in two hours than three weeks of laborious touring of the boondocks on the ground.

A while ago, having heard of some blue-chip property about fifty miles from my home, I called the airport and arranged for a charter plane. Two hours later I returned with not only a comprehensive knowledge of the property involved, but much of the surrounding area. The cost? Only $62!

Maybe you will say, "We can't afford to do that," but consider what gasoline and incidentals, not to mention two or three weeks' time, would cost you. There is also the danger that while you are sightseeing the landowner may lease to someone else.

After you have "tied up" the property, it is time to get down to the nitty-gritty of blind locations, etc., by using a helicopter, hondas, a four-wheel-drive vehicle, or man's earliest mode of transportation — your feet or "shanks mares" as my grandfather used to say.

Property Evaluation

So you have found property that looks good to you? Let's sit down and think about it a bit as there are several things to consider before you actually approach the landowner and try to procure a lease.

The first thing to consider: Is it a good area for waterfowl? The characteristics that make up a good area are easily identified. The location of the water is important. It must be quiet and reasonably secluded. Good cover must prevail. If it is being used for grazing, which many good waterfowl areas are, then be sure it's not overgrazed as you need a reasonable amount of cover.

Some farmers will let you fence off some water areas. Are the ponds shallow? If so, and you have a cold snap, they will freeze and the birds will go elsewhere. If it also has running water or deep lakes then you are all right. Does it have some natural feed? Many properties have native stands of wild rice, wild celery, and sago plant. These, of course, can be planted. If it has no natural feed and it can't be planted you are still all right if it is located in an agricultural area because as long as the birds can feed nearby they will fly to

```
PROPERTY EVALUATION CHECK LIST


PLUSES                              NEGATIVES

Good cover                          Over grazed

Secluded                            Near highway

Running water and lakes             Shallow potholes

Natural feed                        No feed

Good soil suitable for              Soil has high alkaline content
planting

Clean water                         Water accumulation, waste discharge
                                    from food processing plant

Owner lives on property             Absentee owner
minimizing patrolling

Private ownership in                Next to public hunting area
immediate vicinity

Quiet                               San Francisco Airport 3 miles away

Nearest town population - 350       Nearest town population - 40,000

Owner willing to give five          Owner wants lease renewable one
year lease at same fee per          year at a time
year

Good resturants and motels          Thirty-five miles to nearest
nearby                              town

Owners do not hunt                  Owner's two sons hunt everyday
                                    after school

High hills around lake,             Completely flat, birds are 100
good pass shooting                  yards high when going out to feed

Lots of corn and wheat in           Tulip capitol of the U.S.
the area

Sheltered valley, minimum           Tornado warnings given hourly on
winds                               Station WIND
```

it. This is actually a plus as you can pass shoot the birds on the way out as well as when they return. This is actually better in some instances than disturbing the birds on the water itself.

We've looked at all the plus factors; now let's have a look at the negative side of the sheet. If the area is located near a heavily populated city or town you are going to have poaching problems. This is not a large minus but it is a consideration. You'll have to heavily post the property as well as patrol it in order to keep the poachers out.

Next to consider are accesses. If private individuals have easements through the property or alongside it, the easement may have considerable use. This results in the birds being disturbed more than they like. It would be

COURTESY OF EDDIE BAUER

important to procure a plat of the area and see who can legally go through. If federal agencies such as the Bureau of Reclamation have easements through the area, this is not detrimental as they only use it periodically for maintenance, etc. Recent directives from these government agencies prohibit personnel from carrying firearms in their vehicles for sporting purposes.

When you're looking at a plat map make sure no one owns a one-acre island in the middle of your lake as this could disrupt your entire activity. A tract of land next to an interstate highway or within the approach path of an airport, likewise, would not be very desirable because of the noise level. Mr. Mallard likes absolute quiet when he is taking his siesta. Properties next to public hunting areas aren't too groovy for obvious reasons — poaching and noise factors.

In summary, if the pluses outnumber the minuses, I'd contact the owners and see what can be done to work out a lease. On the next page we have printed a checklist which consolidates my thoughts.

Securing a Lease

After you have located a desirable tract, the next step is to find out who owns it. This is rather simple if the owner lives on the property. If no one lives on the property, you'll have to do a little detective work. Get a map of the area; take it to either a surveyor or some agency that might have some activity in that particular area. An example would be the Soil Conservation Agency or Fire District. From them you can obtain the approximate legal description. Armed with this, go to the County Auditor's or the Treasurer's office. The property should be on the tax rolls and they can tell you who owns it.

When you find out who owns the property, then make the approach. Usually a letter is the best method as it gives the landowner a little time to think prior to a face-to-face discussion. Your letter should state the facts as simply as possible. In essence, you and your friends are interested in leasing a hunting area. You should relate to him that you have a light knowledge of their particular tract. Simply say you will call him in a few days to set up a meeting time convenient to him. A sample pre-approach letter is printed on the next page.

When you call the landowner takes on a great deal of significance. There is an old adage in sales that is applicable to just about anything. It states: "Always conduct your interview under favorable circumstances." Do not call the farmer in the middle of July when he is harvesting his wheat. After working fourteen hours a day, he doesn't want his ear bent by a bunch of birdwatchers. The opposite of this would be to get in touch with him about August 15. He has harvested his wheat and if he has had a good crop, chances are he will be in a good frame of mind. If he hasn't had a good crop, he might need the money the lease would generate. Of course, not all landowners are farmers but you can adjust to each situation.

Consummating the lease requires that the two of you come to an arrangement satisfactory to both parties. In Chapter 17, we outline some important guidelines as to the physical lease. The subject of the fee will be a prime consideration to both parties. As costs vary in each section of the country, you'll have to do a little diligent probing to come up with some numbers as to what others are paying. Point out to him money isn't the only consideration. He'll say, "What is then?" You can tell him you'll be responsible for any damage to personal property or livestock losses and that you'll guarantee this by taking out an insurance policy in his favor. If he has had trouble with vandalism or stock being shot, you may have touched his "hot button."

Several years ago I consummated a lease on some property that had never been leased during the fifteen years the owner had it. It had been open to general hunting but as the years passed and the litter grew deeper and the gates were left open allowing his stock to stray, the owner's patience grew thin. The clincher happened when a prime steer was shot. He decided then that he would be better off with a lease where he could hold somebody responsible.

With the help of our outline you may successfully consummate a lease. If the property should turn out to be already leased, in a very gentlemanly manner request that when it comes up for renewal you would like the opportunity to bid on it. The owner may say he is not interested in leasing his property on any basis. All you can do in this case is tell him you'll keep in touch. You should watch for changes in situations and ownership.

PRE-APPROACH LETTER TO PROSPECTIVE LESSOR

Mr. William Smith
Shady Lane Drive
Waseca, Minnesota

Dear Mr. Smith:

With more and more people hunting each year, we've noticed a definite trend in the lack of places to shoot. Several of us have decided to try and find a spot we can lease for ourselves and our families. We've noticed in looking for such a place that you have some lakes on your property. We'd like to discuss the possibility of leasing your land for waterfowl shooting.

I'll call you in a few days to see if we can set up a time convenient to you to discuss this further.

Yours truly,

Barney Birdwatcher

Barney Birdwatcher

Chapter 17
HUNTING LEASES AND HOW TO DRAW THEM

In this chapter, for the benefit of the reader, we have printed an actual hunting lease. The lease covers a great many more subjects than the average person would normally run into. At the same time it covers most of the contingencies you'll become exposed to. I assure you that in twenty years of leasing land, as well as owning some tracts, a great many unusual situations have arisen. Fortunately we've had the capacity to resolve them as they appeared.

Section 1 - Importance of the Lease

I cannot stress too strongly the importance of a lease. In the preceding chapters we have gone through some rather laborious phases in the constructing of blinds and creating waterfowl habitat. We can do all this but it might be for naught if we do not take steps to protect our efforts.

You must draw a good lease; one that is fair to you as the lessee, as well as the lessor. Its provisions must assure you of continuity of hunting and at the same time not cause the landowner to regret the lease.

The lease you have just read will never be found in a legal blank. It represents the culmination of years of problems, experiences and disappointments. Most attorneys have had little or no experience in drawing hunting and fishing leases. Show your attorney this one; it could be of great help to him and he can easily adapt it to your specific needs.

Section 2 - The Analysis of the Lease

A lease should start by stating the names of the persons involved. The person owning the land is referred to as the lessor. The party desiring to lease the land is the lessee. The agreement should give their full identity as well as the city and state of residency. Later, if someone needs to be located, it will make the task easier as many tracts of land are owned by absentee owners.

You will note in the paragraph following "WITNESSETH" we state: "The Lessor does hereby give, grant and lease unto the Lessee the exclusive hunting and fishing rights in, to and upon the land described in Schedule A attached hereto on the terms and conditions hereinafter set forth." The reason we include the word "fishing" is to have control of land in the nonhunting season. Too much activity can disrupt nesting of waterfowl as well as resting birds that use the water areas. In many states fishing seasons run almost into the duck hunting season. If migrant waterfowl are put under too much pressure they will leave. This will have a rather serious effect on your early hunting.

L E A S E

THIS AGREEMENT IS made this 31st day of January, 1972, between:

JOHN B. DOE RANCH, INC. of Seattle, Washington and JOHN B. DOE hereinafter referred to as the Lessor,

and

PAUL S. BERNSEN of Moses Lake, Washington, hereinafter referred to as the Lessee.

W I T N E S S E T H:

The Lessor does hereby give, grant and lease unto the Lessee the exclusive hunting and fishing right in, to and upon the land described in Schedule A attached hereto on the terms and conditions hereinafter set forth.

1. TERM: The term of this lease shall be for a period of three years which shall end at the close of the 1974 migratory waterfowl hunting season. The 1974 migratory waterfowl season would actually terminate on or about January 31, 1975.

2. RENT: The Lessee agrees to pay the Lessor cash rent of $10,000 for the first year, $2,500 per year for the second and third years. The Lease rent shall be paid on April 1, 1972.

3. U.S. WILD LIFE ACT: In the event the United States Department of Interior, Fish and Wildlife Service, in accordance with the International Migratory Waterfowl Treaty, should elect to incept a closure of any hunting season or seasons on waterfowl referred to herein, the Lessor agrees to extend this Lease for a period equal in time to the season or seasons closed.

4. <u>IMPROVEMENTS AND PRACTICES</u>: At its own cost and expense Lessee plans and agrees to:

a. Construct sundry earth fill dams on waste land in order to create additional water covered areas for waterfowl and fill said areas thus created by either pumping or gravity flow, thus adding to existing water resources.

b. Construct permanent hunting blinds consistent with natural surroundings and cover, to be strategically located so as to not conflict with another blind's shooting.

c. Post and patrol the entire tract to reduce poaching and protect the cattle operation which will be concurrently taking place on the premises. Locks will be provided for all gates, with keys or combinations furnished to Lessor, other tenants and authorized federal or state authorities or agencies, e.g. Bonneville Power Administration, etc.

d. Practice regulation and conservation of hunting resources by regulating shooting days and restricting hunting pressure on various hunting areas.

e. It appearing that certain lakes on the property are suitable for planting of trout, Lessee agrees to survey said lakes and to plant trout fish in those lakes considered suitable for planting in order to make fishing available to Lessee and his associates.

5. <u>PERMANENCY OF IMPROVEMENTS</u>: It is agreed that all improvements made by the Lessee shall become the property of

Lessor; that all improvements shall be made at the sole cost and expense of the Lessee; that all improvements, to the extent possible, shall be of permanent nature.

6. INDEMNIFICATION OF LESSOR: Lessee agrees to hold Lessor harmless from any accident or liability arising out of an accident on the property and will provide the necessary insurance for that purpose.

7. ASSIGNING AND SUBLEASING: It is agreed that Lessee may assign and/or sublease portions of or the entire premises, but Lessee shall still remain liable for payment of the rent and observance of the covenants in the event of a sublease or assignment.

8. SUCCESSORS: This lease shall bind the parties hereto, their successors and assigns.

IN WITNESS WHEREOF, the parties hereto have hereunto set their hand and seals the day and year first above written.

JOHN B. DOE RANCH, INC.

BY: _John B. Doe_

PAUL S. BERNSEN

Paul S Bernsen

JOHN B. DOE

John B. Doe

AGREEMENT AND RIGHT OF FIRST REFUSAL

For valuable consideration received, the undersigned, John B. Doe (the "grantor") hereby agrees to grant and does grant to Paul S. Bernsen, or his assigns, the following rights. The rights granted hereby shall exist and expire concurrently with the term of that certain lease between the parties hereto dated January 31, 1972.

If the grantor shall receive any bonafide offer for the purchase of the grantor's interest in the property described in said lease, such offer shall not be accepted unless the same offer shall have been made and delivered to Bernsen or his assigns in writing and shall not have been accepted in accordance with its terms within thirty (30) days after the date of such delivery.

The right of first refusal shall not apply to any offer, sale or transfer involving less than the total acreage of the John B. Doe Ranch, Inc., together with the grantor's total interest under the real estate contract dated October 29, 1969, which contract is described in said lease.

Dated this 31st day of January, 1972.

_____
JOHN B. DOE

_____
PAUL S. BERNSEN

STATE OF WASHINGTON)
)SS
County of King   )

On the 31st day of January, 1972, before me, the undersigned, a Notary Public in and for the State of Washington,
duly commissioned and sworn, personally appeared John B. Doe
to me known to be the President of John B. Doe Ranch, Inc.,
the corporation that executed the foregoing instrument, and
acknowledged the said instrument to be the free and voluntary
act and deed of said corporation, for the uses and purposes
therein mentioned, and on oath stated that he was authorized
to execute the said instrument and that the seal affixed is the
corporate seal of said corporation.

Witness my hand and official seal hereto affixed the day
and year first above written.

Henry Smith
Notary Public in and for the State
of Washington, residing at Redmond

STATE OF WASHINGTON)
)SS
County of King   )

On this day personally appeared before me John B. Doe to
me known to be the individual described in and who executed the
within the foregoing instrument, and acknowledged that he signed
the same as his free and voluntary act and deed, for the uses
and purposes therein mentioned.

GIVEN under my hand and official seal this 31st day of
January, 1972.

Henry Smith
Notary Public in and for the State of
Washington, residing in Redmond

ALL IN TOWNSHIP 13 NORTH, RANGE 31 EAST, WILLAMETTE MERIDIAN:

PARCEL A: All of Section 2

PARCEL B: All of Section 3

PARCEL C: All of Section 4

PARCEL D: All of Section 5

PARCEL E: All of Section 6 except Farm Unit 114

PARCEL F: All of Section 7

PARCEL G: All of Section 8

PARCEL H: All of Section 9

PARCEL I: All of Section 10

PARCEL J: All of Section 17

PARCEL K: That portion of Section 18 as owned by the Lessor
            according to the plat thereof recorded in the office
            of the Auditor of Franklin County, Washington

ALL IN TOWNSHIP 14 NORTH, RANGE 30 EAST, WILLAMETTE MERIDIAN:

PARCEL L: All of Section 25

Second but still quite important in including the fishing rights in the lease is the financial aspect. You may have an abundance of bait on the property such as water dogs, minnows and hellgrammites all of which can be sold at good prices and the profit can be used to defray the cost of your lease, blind construction, etc. We will now break down the individual sections that make up the lease.

1. *TERM*: The section covering term spells out the length of time the lease is to run as well as any provision to renew the lease.

2. *RENT*: This section covers the amount to be paid each year and when it is due. In the lease illustrated between John B. Doe and myself, I agreed to pay Mr. Doe more money in the first year than in the second and third years. This was an inducement for him to execute the lease. He was in a short cash position and the idea of getting most of the money up front appealed to him.

3. *U.S. WILDLIFE ACT*: This provision is just a safety valve. In the event the Department of Interior would enact a closure of the duck hunting season, this automatically extends the lease for the period of the closure.

Although a closure is unlikely, it is still a possibility and should be incorporated into each lease particularly if you are prepaying the lease.

4. *IMPROVEMENTS AND PRACTICES*: In this paragraph of the lease you state what you intend to do with the property as to blind construction, lake creation, planting of duck food and cover. This all comes under your interest. As to the landowner, he will be interested in your posting, patrolling and gate erections. You may want permission to fence the areas you have planted with duck food. If all these things are spelled out at the time the lease is negotiated you'll have no subsequent problems.

5. *PERMANENCY OF IMPROVEMENTS*: Here we state that the improvements we have made revert to the owner at the conclusion of the lease. Care must be exercised that we don't do too much construction on short-term leases as it is impossible to amortize a heavy expenditure over a three-year lease. By the same token, if you plan to erect a nice clubhouse make sure it is movable. As to blinds, most of them can be moved with a little engineering on the part of the construction team. In Chapter 2, we expound on this at some length.

6. *INDEMNIFICATION OF LESSOR*: All this boils down to is your furnishing an insurance policy naming the Lessor as an additional insured which relieves him from the liability aspect of an accident or incident occurring on his property. Normal coverage would be $300,000 per person/$300,000 per occurrence. This should be adequate. The cost of this is quite modest and affords the Lessor considerable peace of mind.

7. *ASSIGNING AND SUBLEASING*: Definitely one of the most important sections of the Lease. Should the shooting go to pot you might want to sublease to another group and relieve yourself of the financial burden. In the case of an exceptionally large tract it might take several groups to fund the cost. You can sublease parts of it and keep the most desirable portion yourself. Several times I've leased tracts of ground only to have a better one turn up in which case I subleased the initial tract, usually at a profit.

In the event of poor health on the part of a Lessee he would definitely want to be able to assign the lease. In the same train of thought, a father might want to convey it to his son. This provision gives him the vehicle to accomplish this.

8. *SUCCESSORS*: In the event the property is sold, this binds the purchaser on the same terms and conditions as the original Lessor. In other words the purchaser has bought the property subject to the lease. Also if you assign or sublease your initial lease, this binds the Lessors to the same terms and conditions that were applicable to you.

Finally, the instrument should be signed by the Lessor and Lessee and notarized. The lease together with Schedule A which describes the leased land should be filed with the County Auditor in the county in which the land is located. It then becomes a matter of public record and represents a legal encumbrance against the property and serves to protect your interest.

Section 3 - Analysis of Agreement and First Right of Refusal

As an addendum to the hunting lease you will note that we have included an instrument called "Agreement and Right of First Refusal." This is a very powerful instrument as it gives you the right to purchase the property you are leasing on the same terms and conditions as any other party making an offer. In a case where you have had the property for some time and know its full recreational value as well as its non-recreational value, it is highly advantageous to have this instrument. Most landowners are reluctant to convey these rights to the Lessee. However, if you have been fortunate enough to have renewed the lease at least once you have probably gained the landlord's confidence and shouldn't be reluctant to ask for it.

Early in my hunting career I lost a couple of blue-chip leases. The land was purchased by big money combines. As an old German friend once said, "Ve get too smart, too late! Ya!"

Heading south.

Mississippi Flyway

Atlantic Flyway

148

Chapter 18
IMPROVING WATERFOWL HABITAT AND SHOOTING CONDITIONS

Section 1 - Creating Water Areas

Many of us fail to realize what we have been blessed with, for all around us lie situations that, if effectively harnessed, can result in a substantial increase in the amount of ducks that we kill. In order to do this we must first examine our own property and determine what we can do to make it a better hunting area. For example, a pothole in the spring might have plenty of water; if the summer evaporation reduces the amount of water in the pond, it may become apparent that by early fall the pothole will be entirely dry. But we can make this a lasting shooting area simply by putting a dam in the lake's exit.

In most places the water will have a natural drain which will exist in the form of a draw or arroyo. By hiring the services of a bulldozer you can put in an earth-filled dam of enough height to sustain and hold back the water. A blue-chip pond can be made at a cost of only a couple hundred dollars and some effort on the part of the members of your duck club. With a pond you'll find that the local hatch will improve substantially and in addition you'll have a spot for the northern ducks to light in when on their southern migration.

I would like to relate a story as to why there is virture in installing Dams. Many years ago a particular lake on one of our properties was suddenly swarming with thousands of ducks and geese. The lake had not gone dry, as it had in the past seasons, because of a cool summer. The following season however it went dry again whereupon we put a dam in the draw and pumped water from another lake about a half mile away. This worked so successfully and at such a small cost that we pumped it full every year thereafter.

The reason for the success of this particular lake can be attributed to the fact that this was an exact duplication of the Canadian Prairie Province potholes where many of the ducks and geese were hatched. The shores of the lake were completely flat and made it a physical impossibility for the birds to be "snuck" up on. As a result of our efforts and a very small expenditure in the cost of the dam, this particular lake produced in excess of fifty geese and several hundred ducks during the course of each season that followed. To make good duck and goose hunting you must be willing to analyze, spend a little money and do a little work.

Fifteen-acre lake created with a little duck hunter's ingenuity.

While the lake is dry, before the installation of the dam takes place, it's an excellent opportunity to install what we refer to as tank blinds. These are blinds that are installed in the bottom of the lake at such a position to allow the birds to be cut off on their departure from the immediate scene of the shooting. For example, the birds in departing a lake will always go out with the wind because this affords them additional momentum in their excitement to leave the area. In Chapter 2, in which we discussed blinds in great detail, you will find an illustration of a tank blind of which there can be several types and modifications.

The trick in installing the blind is to make sure that it is in exactly the right location. Birds are great creatures of habit and will leave a lake in precisely the same place depending on the prevailing wind. The blinds should be located in a place that will take advantage of this. We refer to a blind located with the prevailing wind as a cutoff blind. After the birds have been shot from other blinds that border the lake, they will then attempt to exit the lake by the prevailing wind. These birds have originally been decoyed in and, at the point of departure, don't have much momentum or altitude so they afford extremely good shots on departing. A blind located under these particular conditions will generally outproduce any other individual blind on the rest of the lake. The effort you put forth in the installation of this type blind can be very rewarding.

After the cutoff blind has been installed and the dam has been completed, the next consideration is the overflow. In an area where you are faced with fast runoffs it is important that an overflow be installed to allow the dam some relief from the impounded waters. The best location of the overflow can be determined by shooting the elevations with a surveyor's instrument. With the use of this instrument you can calculate how much lower the overflow should be in relation to the top of the dam. When the water reaches the level of the overflow, rather than put pressure on the dam, it will flow out. Thus you will take the pressure off the dam and as soon as the input stops, the lake will remain at a constant level. The level of the overflow should be consistent with the elevation of water in relationship to the installed blinds. Be careful and be sure at this point, that on a day of high winds the water will not get high enough to slop into the blind. Nothing is more uncomfortable than a wet derriere.

Between the installation of the tank blinds and the installation of the dam and overflow, the total cost would not be over several hundred dollars. When you amortize this over the years of use it becomes very low in cost and the results will be well worth it.

Section 2 - Planting of Feed

There are many other things that can be done to improve waterfowl habitat as well as the shooting conditions. One of the main ones being the planting of feed. When you have a good body of water the birds are obviously using it for two reasons: (1) to get a drink; and (2) as a place to rest. The availability of feed is the third inducement which you can have some control over.

There are many fine duck foods among which there are sago plant, giant wild rice, wild celery and millet. There are over forty varieties of duck food available for all conditions. Most plants can be raised in both the North and the South and are readily acclimated to your particular conditions. There are several suppliers of duck foods in business right now, one of whom is John Lemberger who owns Wildlife Nurseries, P.O. Box 399-D, Oshkosh, Wisconsin 54901. Many of you have probably seen his advertisements in some of the outdoor publications. I have personally tried many of his plants and found them to be quite satisfactory. If you'll send Wildlife Nurseries a soil sample of the land in which the plant is to be acclimated, they will do a soil analysis and advise you as to what will be suitable to your area.

One of the newer innovations to the market is wild Japanese millet which can be obtained from Gunnersfield Enterprises, Inc., P.O. Box 626, Maxwell, California 95955. In addition to the food qualities of this wild Japanese millet, it also provides excellent cover for all game birds and is alkali tolerant. Many areas have a tendency to go a little alkaline when water is placed on them. This wild Japanese millet is also flood and drought resistant and is highly productive. It will produce up to two thousand pounds of seed per acre and is self-reseeding so it is not necessary to replant it each year.

Wild Japanese millet.

Contrary to public opinion in the planting of wild rice, it is necessary that the body of water to be planted have both an inlet and an outlet because wild rice will not grow in stagnated water. Most people in planting wild rice have a tendency to "broadcast the seed, that is throw it liberally over the surface of the lake. All you accomplish is to feed the ducks and geese because after your departure they will dive for the seed and eat it, resulting in no crop. To avoid this you can buy some cheesecloth and cut it into 4-inch squares. Place the seeds in a ball of mud, place the ball of mud in the cheesecloth and then tie the top so that you have a parachute-like apparatus, and heave these cheesecloth balls around the lake. The idea here is to prevent the ducks and geese from eating the seed. The seed will sink to the bottom of the lake in the mud ball and later germinate. The best time to plant is late spring after the ducks and geese have gone north. This will enable your crop to get a good growth on the bottom of the lake and you'll surely have good shooting in the fall. Although this may sound like a great deal of work, it is a sure-fire method of getting a crop.

All of the firms that offer duck foods have specific instructions enclosed with the order so that even a neophyte, if he follows the instructions explicitly, can accomplish some good.

Section 3 - Water Control

In many parts of the country the average sportsman has available to him certain usages of water. By this I mean that some of you may be able to pump water from rivers that flow by your property. Usually ducks are reluctant to light on fast-moving water except in extremely cold conditions;

Lake overflow to relieve dam pressure. This was blasted through solid rock to eliminate "washing."

however, they will readily use small ponds and lakes that are heavily brushed.

How do you get the water from the river or stream into the interior of your property? Really quite simply! The water can be pumped by two methods: (1) by the use of an electric pump, and (2) by the use of a gasoline-powered pump. If there is no electricity available, there are many very efficient gasoline-operated pumps that will pump water the required distance from the river.

Probably the most efficient method of pumping water in remote locations where there is no electricity available is by the use of the tractor. Most modernday tractors have what is known as a power takeoff. This power takeoff can be hooked up to a pump which need not be submerged. The engine will pump water over a great distance without an appreciable friction loss. I have personally used a power takeoff tractor-operated pump that pumped water for a mile and at a lift of seventy-five feet. This type of pump, with an initial capacity of 1,000 gallons per minute, can pump water for a mile and at a lift of seventy-five feet and will still end up pumping 700 gallons per minute despite the friction loss in both the length and the elevation. The use of gasoline is quite economical, so economical that I have filled a ten-acre lake in five days of pumping at a cost of only $225 in consumed gasoline. The total gallonage pumped was three million gallons.

Most implement dealers will rent a tractor for $25 per day and the whole concept here is not to make a great body of water but rather a shallow one which the birds like. This is particularly true if the time of year is such that there is still enough warmth left in the ground that new grass will sprout after the water is put on it. Birds will flock in as ducks and geese like nothing better than the new green grass. Although ducks and geese love grain, they must have some roughage in their diet. Roughage consists of grasses that can be grown in flooded areas, provided you are favored by the weather.

The best type of irrigation pipe to use is aluminum which is light in weight and easily transported to the site. Six-inch pipe is the best dimension as it is the most common and seems to get the job done best. Most irrigation companies will rent 6-inch irrigation pipe at a cost of ten cents per foot per week. If you were to rent 2,500 feet of pipe which would be approximately a half mile and you felt the body of water could be pumped full in one week then you would have a cost of $250 for the pipe rental. Pumping water a half mile probably is the extreme example because there will be many situations where it is only necessary to pump water a couple hundred feet or a couple hundred yards. In addition to this, if the terrain is such that the water will run by gravity, it is possible that you may be able to dike and fill several ponds at the same time.

In areas where most of the farming is done by irrigation, it is not at all necessary to even get involved in pumping water via the use of power takeoff tractors, etc. You can make ponds simply by finding a spot which lies below the irrigation ditch and water can be siphoned out via gravity and run down into the depression you intend to fill. This is particularly advantageous shortly before the irrigation water is turned off for the season because you

Before dam installation.

again have the availability of the new grass which the birds like so well. In the Western United States most irrigation districts stop transmitting water about October 25th so it would be good to start filling your pond around the 5th of October. This is usually a few days before the opening of the hunting season and will allow the lake ample time to fill. In many irrigation districts there is considerable waste water. The waste water is collected in what is commonly called "wasteways" and transported into another reservoir. However, there are many stops and exits for the water before it ever hits the parent wasteway. If on your particular tract of ground the wasteway passes through, you may again siphon the water off and use this to irrigate a crop of your own planting. If this situation exists, the use of the water can serve several purposes. If you plant a crop the water can be used to irrigate until such time as the grain is ready. Then at this point, after the blinds are installed, you can flood the area. This will attract ducks by the thousands and you will once again enjoy super shooting.

In summary, the many points we have covered so far in this chapter, concerning the creation of a waterfowl habitat, are merely ideas but are some of the things we have experienced through the years that we have found very helpful in increasing our duck yield and providing additional nesting and resting areas for birds. You must however think of each situation as being individual and try to find a solution that utilizes resources at hand, namely the water or terrain. With this in mind you can take what formerly was a barren area, void of ducks, and turn it into one that will be wonderful hunting.

Section 4 — Agriculture and Waterfowl

With the vast amounts of urban development as well as the industrial usage of former waterfowl nesting sites, the birds have lost some of their natural feeding areas. They have replaced these areas with a dependency on agriculture. If we were to delete agriculture, the present population of ducks and geese would not survive. The birds have become so accustomed to using man's agricultural products that they are reliant on a certain amount of grain and grass to make up their diet.

The modern-day duck hunter who is fortunate enough to live on a migration flyway should attempt to either purchase or lease agricultural lands for the purpose of shooting migrant waterfowl. The most desirable tracts are those that are located close in proximity to game refuges or large bodies of water. The birds feel safer being close to refuges and the larger bodies of water.

The prices for leasing on some of these tracts usually is quite high; however, if a group of compatible individuals band together, the cost of the lease can be divided among them. This helps to bring the cost to a level that the participants can all afford. If your group is fortunate enough to either be able to lease one of these tracts or purchase one, then the next step to consider is the appropriate blind.

When you have plenty of feed, you can go one step further in your quest for the illusive Mallard or goose and arrange to have the fields flooded. You will be surprised how much the addition of water will improve your shooting. The conditions that enable you to flood a field after the crop has been harvested usually are common to the rice fields of Texas, California and Louisiana. Some of the wheat fields in Canada and the Western United States are also easily flooded. Again this comes to the point that the individual should see what practical application he can make to his own environment. The rewards will be most gratifying.

Is this water wasted?

No! Water is impounded by dam at west end of swamp creating twenty acres of duck habitat.

Flooded wheat field loaded with geese. You can do it too!

Chapter 19
RUNNING A DUCK CLUB

The most important part of a duck club is its leadership. Even the best property can be rendered useless unless it is properly administered. The club's leader must be strong as well as fair. There will be many occasions when some internal squabble will arise. These situations must be mediated and settled in the best interest of the club. Decisions must be made that will affect the entire group and made without hesitation. He will have to negotiate leases and in some instances sign them personally. Many landowners only want to deal with an individual. All these items call for an extraordinary person. Select him carefully!

Club Administration
Members

The number of members depends on two prime factors:

1. The size of the property will determine how many shooters it will support. This should be done very prudently as there is no rule of thumb but rather depends on the number of ducks and how much shooting pressure the property will stand.

2. The second factor is cost. If the lease is very expensive you'll have to take in more members to fund it than you would need with a cheaper tract.

Another thing to take into account is the age of the members. The older ones won't hunt as hard as the young ones. The weather takes its toll of participation interest. Some of the members can only hunt in fixed cycles. An example would be doctors who are very restricted in their leisure time. Build the composition of your group around a wide cross section of people.

Guests

This is a sore subject in many clubs and a difficult one to handle. Everyone has definite ideas. It is one area where you have to put some teeth in the rules. Our format on guests took a long time to develop but has worked quite satisfactorily now that it is in force. It works this way:

First Week — No guests

Weekends Thereafter — Guests every other weekend one (1) at a time

Weekdays Thereafter — Wednesdays and Thursdays one (1) guest at a time

Holiday Vacations — One guest per day usually restricted to immediate family members. (Thanksgiving and Christmas)

Many clubs have both husbands and wives who hunt. The only solution to this is to have them both buy memberships. In this way if they have sons or daughters who hunt, each can bring a guest which resolves their togetherness problem. Your "fearless leader" has to be a tough taskmaster in the area of guest violations.

Shooting Days

Again this calls for scheduling. We've tried many formulas and the one that has worked best for us is as follows:

First Week — The property is open everyday

Subsequent Weeks — Wednesdays, Thursdays, Saturdays and Sundays

Holiday Vacations — The property is open every day of the vacation

Last Three Weeks of the Season — The property is open everyday

Property Rotation

If the property is large enough, the shooting areas within it can be rotated. For example, part of the lakes or potholes can be shot on Wednesday. The other part can be shot on Thursday. The first parcel you shot would come up in rotation on Saturday and the second parcel would be available again for Sunday shooting.

You cannot hammer the property day in and day out. An exception to this might be if the property were located next to a game refuge where it might stand the pressure during the height of the migration.

If you are fortunate enough to have two different leases, you can shoot one tract on Wednesday and Thursday; then shoot the other tract on Saturday and Sunday. In this way each property would get a week's rest between shoots.

Between sound management on your shooting days schedule and good property rotation, the bird population on your property will build up substantially. Birds will become less wary and your production will increase sharply. If you practice both of these concepts, you will truly be able to SHOOT LESS AND GET MORE!

Work Parties

"Work parties" is a carry-over term from GI days. It means the assembling of troups to perform a particular task. In its application to a duck club it means getting all the members together in order to get the property functional and ready for the coming hunting season. It becomes fairly obvious that unless you are giving a new shotgun away for a door prize, you won't get them all there at one time.

The remedy to this is not too complicated. Work parties are normally scheduled on weekends. However, some of the members won't be able to come on weekends but could work during the week. At this point the club leader should appoint several captains. Each captain will take a different day and be responsible for getting the members working that day to the site and accomplishing their phase of the work program.

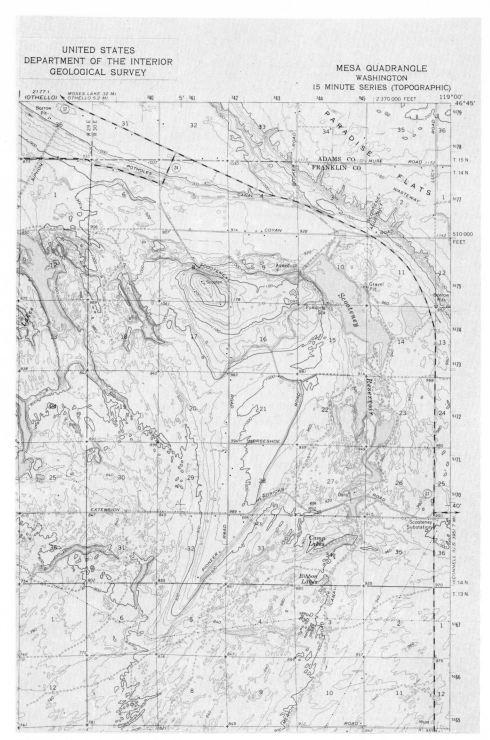

Portion of United States Quadrangle Map

The Work

Reflecting on our old GI days, we all recall standing around until someone got us in motion, usually with a cursory remark. With the threat of the stockade removed, the club members won't be too impressed by yelling and shouting. Instead be well organized. In the role of a "field marshall" for many years, I found we were 200 percent more efficient by having a work party before the work party. The captains and I would get together the day before the scheduled work party and get all the first stages done, such as:

1. Cut and haul brush or tules to the blind sites.
2. Strip all the old camouflage from the blinds and haul it away.
3. If new blinds were to be assembled and installed, have them at the site.
4. Boats that needed painting were out and ready to be painted.
5. All posting materials were boxed and ready for posting teams to distribute.

By doing these things in advance we lost a minimum of time. Shortly before the work party a bulletin went out to each member advising him to bring the following items: shovel, ax, pliers, hammer, boots, bug repellent, hat, drinking water and lunch.

On the day of the work party we divided the work party into teams:

1. Blind camouflage team
2. Boat maintenance team
3. Posting team
4. Blind assembly team

The secret to a successful work party is having everyone doing something.

You should assign the older members to the less strenuous tasks. In having work parties, press all the people you can into service. If members' wives and children hunt, they should also help on the work parties. The kids are enthusiastic and make excellent workers. Having a work party helps familiarize the members with the property and makes them appreciative of what they have.

Maps

It's a good idea to have a map of your property. I suggest you get one which has been done by some federal or state agency. The best of these are the Quadrangle maps. They show in detail different quadrangles of each county. Outlined in the maps are all the water areas as well as roads. The cost of each map is usually about $1.00. Each member should have one so he can mark the location of all blinds on the property. Quadrangle maps are available by writing to the U.S. Geological Survey, Denver, Colorado 80225. To show how definitive the quadrangle maps are we've printed a portion of one here.

Meetings

In your club functions it is a good idea to have at least two meetings a year. The first one should be a business meeting at which time you can iron out problems and discuss new development work and other ideas of general interest to the group. The second meeting should be social with the wives invited, particularly if they don't hunt. It gives them a better feel for all of your absent weekends.

Chapter 20
POSTING, FENCING AND PATROLLING YOUR PROPERTY

You can have the finest property in the world, build the best blinds and the fanciest spread of decoys, but it won't do a bit of good unless you can keep the poachers off!

Section 1 — Posting

In order to keep them off your property it's necessary to heavily post the property. Your sign must have some "bite" to it in order for them to get the message. Later in this chapter we have printed several signs we have found to be effective.

The Signs

Ink fades and this should be given consideration in having signs printed. Lettering done in black will last the longest. We have tried various gaudy colors only to have them fade from sun and rain. We finally settled on a white sign with black print.

Cost of Signs

If you buy signs in small lots the unit cost is quite high, around $.15 per sign. If you order signs printed especially for your own use you can reduce the cost quite sharply. In lots of 1,000 or more the unit cost drops to about $.04 per sign which is quite reasonable. With the use of weather-resistant paper and black print a sign has a life expectancy of about four years. You will, of course, loose a few each year to poachers.

Effective poacher control. Heavy posting of Powder River Gate and good fencing.

Posting Materials

The most economical material to staple the sign on is 1/4-inch exterior plywood. The plywood is cut into pieces that are slightly larger than the signs. The signs we use are eight inches wide by twelve inches long. The signs are made out of heavy-duty, weather-resistant paper. The plywood board is slightly larger than the sign itself. When the sign is centered and stapled on it leaves a border. You can have a lumberyard cut the plywood pieces for about $.08 each. When the sign needs replacing it is a simple matter to rip the old sign off and replace it with a new one.

Preparing the Signs and Installing Them

First staple the signs to the boards. Then drill them and affix a lightweight wire to them for the purpose of tying the sign to the fencing wires. We used to drill only two holes, one on each side at the top of the sign. We then fastened the wire to a strand on the fence. However, this allowed the sign to swing freely in the wind and it was only a matter of time before one or both of the wires holding the sign broke, thus undoing all of our labor.

To overcome this problem we drilled four holes, one in each corner. With a long bit as many as twenty boards can be drilled at one time. The holes should be large enough so that the wire passes through easily but small enough to reduce the wind give. Next we put the wires through the holes, one in each corner, and wound them as tightly as possible around the fencing wires — the top two to the wire of the fence above and the lower two to the strand below. This resulted in a nice snug job with no wind give and, of course, fewer fallen signs.

In preparing the signs, divide your members into teams — one group stapling the signs on the boards, another drilling, a third affixing the wires and, of course, another putting them on the fence.

Frequency of Signs

Normally every 100 yards is effective enough. However, the laws of your state may require more than that to be legal. In areas along highways, particularly where your water is visible, it may be necessary to have signs up at even more frequent intervals.

Where to Post

Your signs should cover the entire boundary of your property. Because of road easements and right-of-ways it is usually more practical to concede that part involving the easements and start your posting.

In the Western United States and Canada almost all land is fenced. This makes posting considerably easier as the signs can either be nailed on fence posts or hung on wires. I prefer to hang them on wires as most modern fencing involves the use of metal fence posts. Telephone or power transmission poles are also good.

Proper posting.

NO TRESPASSING

KEEP OUT
RESTRICTED
AREA

PRIVATE
GUN CLUB
No Trespassing

Patroled Property
No Trespassing
Violators will be
Prosecuted

No Hunting
CATTLE COUNTRY

COMMON POSTING SIGNS

Even if you want to deviate from my 100-yard-interval formula you should try to place the sign where it is clearly visible. Avoid brush and tall grass. Instead select knolls and high ridges. Placing it in a swale is a waste of money.

Shortcuts to Posting

Posting should be done in teams — each team should take a specific area. Using a pickup, one person can drive and the others can sit on the tailgate, taking turns jumping off and installing the signs. If you divide the property by north, south, east and west boundaries, no one is going to be terribly overworked and you can post a rather large area in a relatively short time. The older members should drive or take the easier terrain.

Posting Unfenced Areas

If you should have an area that's unfenced, you need only take the signs we have discussed, staple them on the plywood boards and nail them to a 4-foot lathe. They can either be dug in or driven in around the boundary of the property. After the season is over they should be picked up and stored until next season. If you leave them out cattle or the wind will knock them down.

Section 2 — Fencing and Gates

Sometimes it's practical to erect your own fences as a poacher deterrent. This is particularly true if you have some nice terrain to work with, such as a small box canyon or a stream that can't be forded. Taking advantage of such a situation only calls for a small amount of fencing, sometimes under 100 yards, which makes the cost quite reasonable.

A gate will probably be needed. The best type of gates are the ones known as Powder River Gates. They are made of steel and are quite durable. They come in different sizes and if there are other users of the property, the gates should be large enough to allow them entry. A large cattle-hauling truck would require a 14-foot gate.

When you install gates you need locks and chain. Padlocks that require keys are not practical if there are too many users. We use Sesame locks which only require dialing the combination. Each padlock comes equipped with a "key" which when inserted in the opened lock allows the combination to be changed which we do frequently. The chain should be fairly substantial or the poachers will come along and cut it off with bolt cutters.

Section 3 — Patrolling the Property

If a poacher can get away with it he'll actually hunt a property until he gets caught, which is sometimes a long time. If your property is well posted, fenced and has locked gates you have a few things going for you that will reduce poaching.

Patrolling the property will hold poachers down to about 5 percent. There is still the individual who was "born free" and he's going to poach anyway. He's the one you have to watch out for. If you are only shooting your area certain days of the week, your work is easier because you know that if you hear shooting it's not one of your group. Each vehicle involved in your group should have a decal displayed somewhere. That way you'll have no trouble determining if you have a poacher or not.

Spotting Poachers

When you're looking for poachers find the highest vantage point that gives you the best view of your property. It's a good idea to have some high-powered binoculars with you. When you spot a poacher proceed immediately to the scene. With first offenders you should be polite but firm. Inform them that they are trespassing and ask them to leave. Always carry a pocket note pad. Jot down their license plate numbers. If they offer any resistance tell them you're going to call the sheriff.

I know one group who carries walkie-talkies. When they run into a poacher they have a great verbal exchange between each other. This has very good psychological effects on the poacher.

Preventative Measures

We have discussed first offenders that we've talked to personally. Then there are those whose vehicles you find. We again jot down their license plate numbers and slip a preprinted note under their windshield wipers. The note informs them that they are trespassing and that another violation will result in the removal of the valve stems from their tires. We don't have too many second offenders. Most poachers aren't in favor of long walks.

An effective method of poacher control which is particularly effective on weekends is to have one member drive around the property at regular intervals. At trouble points, such as gates, we have erected large signs stating that unauthorized vehicles will be towed away to such and such a town. This has proven to be quite effective. There are many ways to deter poachers and if you maintain a constant vigil they'll soon look for better poaching grounds.

Epilog — "The Saga of Harry Honda"

Several years ago when Hondas became quite popular, one sophisticated poacher who we nicknamed "Harry" decided he could adapt the use of a Honda to his activities. For several years he gave us fits, running all over the property, shooting everything up.

He was just like the phantom, always one step ahead of us. It got to be a game. We'd spend countless hours waiting for him and he'd always show up elsewhere on the ranch.

Sometimes we'd get fleeting glimpses of him riding hell-bent for election through the dingleberries. Somehow he always got away.

We finally decided to booby-trap him. We looked for places where he entered the ranch and narrowed it down to about three points. His poaching route took him from north to south on one trip and south to north on another.

Because in taking these routes he had to pass over these three points we decided to put the booby traps there. We warned all the club members of the hazards and told them to avoid the areas. As the three points were all on our property the chances of any outsiders getting involved were nonexistent.

"Harry the Honda" would lift his bike over the fence or push it underneath; then ride up his "own" trail and begin harassing the ducks. His route took him about four miles. Then he would leave the ranch to be picked up by a confederate.

At each of the three points we installed a booby trap consisting of a board with several dozen nails driven through it. We then concealed the board, nails up, by sifting sand over it. "Harry" even evaded these for a while. Then one day we got him. At this particular place he had to make a pretty good run at a hill. Going that fast he couldn't see what was concealed on the lip of the hill. The board lodged in his tire and he spilled in the sand.

Duck shooting got pretty good after that. We saw no sign of "Harry" and figured he'd learned his lesson. However, the other day I was checking fences near one of our duck ponds and much to my amazement there was a Honda track! Would you believe — "Son of Harry the Honda"!

Chapter 21
CLOTHING AND ACCESSORIES

The clothing worn in waterfowl shooting must be multi-purposed. It must be dry and warm and yet not be too hot when the weather is mild. It must not restrict your movements when walking and it must have some built-in camouflage qualities. We have printed a color and clothing systems chart at the end of this chapter. While the items in the systems may not cover every unknown, it will cover most of the situations and conditions.

COLD WEATHER

Outer Garments

Hunting Coats — When the mercury dips, it's important that you're warm enough. In cold weather a basic hunting coat will not keep you warm enough nor should you expect it to. To date the warmest insulation against cold is down. In a properly fabricated garment you can be comfortable far below zero. Your shooting coat should be roomy enough so that you can slip a vest or sweater underneath. Two layers of clothing will create an "airspace" and have a better warming effect than one layer. The pockets should be large enough to carry at least a box of shells, matches and extra gloves.

Down Shooting Coat
Courtesy Eddie Bauer, Inc.
Seattle, Washington

Ironclad Field Pants
Courtesy Eddie Bauer, Inc.
Seattle, Washington

Pants — Most cold-weather shooting does not involve getting your pants wet, you are restricted to shooting big water, fields or jump shooting creeks or streams. Therefore, you have the walking element to contend with. There's nothing worse than sitting in a tumbleweed blind in a corn or wheat field and getting continually "pricked" by the cover you're sitting in. There's only one solution — pants that have a hard finish. Hard-finished pants are double-layered and have a hard fabric over a soft one. They are the ticket for plowing through briers, thorns, tumbleweeds, etc. In addition, if you're jump shooting without a dog, you can always slip a pair of boots or waders over them.

Inner Garments

In the case of inner garments in cold weather, you have a little bit more flexibility. Thermal or down underwear will keep you nice and warm. Long johns or "woolies" also do a good job. Care should be exercised in the purchase of "woolies" or long johns. If you have sensitive skin, you may be subjecting yourself to considerable itching and irritation. Many western loggers, however, wear "woolies" because even if they get wet they'll stay warm.

You should wear two pairs of socks — an inner lightweight pair to absorb perspiration and provide additional warmth and an outer pair either wool or thermal. Walking long distances in cold weather causes your feet to perspire and can be serious if you don't allow for it. The socks should be high enough to eliminate their sliding down. They can also be "bloused" over the lower portion of your pants.

Downlight Under Garments
Courtesy Eddie Bauer, Inc.
Seattle, Washington

Two-ply Thermal Underwear
Courtesy Eddie Bauer, Inc.
Seattle, Washington

Arctic Cap
Courtesy Eddie Bauer, Inc.
Seattle, Washington

Botte Sauvage Lace Boots
Courtesy Gokey Company
St. Paul, Minnesota

Navy Frogman Mitts
Courtesy Eddie Bauer, Inc.
Seattle, Washington

Footwear

Proper footwear becomes very important in cold weather because you can't afford to end up with wet feet. If you're sitting in a blind on big water, then insulated foot-pacs or hiking boots with wool socks will do the trick. But, if you're out jump shooting or putting decoys out in a stream, you'll need insulated hip boots or waders depending on the water depth. When you're wearing hip boots or waders, it's important to keep your stockings "bloused" under your pants because if they slip down, your feet will get cold and you'll chafe the skin off your ankles and legs. Garters will also eliminate the sock-slipping problem.

Accessories

Your hat or cap should be warm to the point you're comfortable. It should have earflaps to protect your ears in extremely cold weather. You can also buy wool, hooded-type face masks. These are excellent in sub-zero temperatures. You'll need two sets of gloves. One pair to put out and take in decoys. The Navy-type frogman gloves are one of the best for running a decoy operation. You should have warm shooting gloves. They shouldn't be too bulky as they'll restrict you when it comes time to pull the trigger. I personally prefer to wear warm shooting gloves, then slip them off when it's time to shoot.

Because most cold-weather garments don't have game compartments built in them, you'll need a game vest. You can also use the vest to carry extra shells, a thermos, additional gloves and many other requirements of the day.

171

MILD WEATHER

Outer Garments

Hunting Coats — When the temperature is in the 35° to 60° range, you'll want a durable lightweight hunting coat with a game compartment to carry the birds in. These coats usually have a hard finish like the traditional duck fabric. The hard finish will protect your arms and shoulders from being scratched.

Hunting Pants or Suits — The best hunting pants are again hard-finished ones. In recent years several companies have gone into making one-piece hunting suits. They are cover-all types and usually have a fabric blend of cotton-dacron in the exterior fabric. The inside lining has a variety of materials.

These one-piece suits are excellent in early fall and are good in the milder climates. Those with thermal and down linings are good all hunting season, in cooler areas.

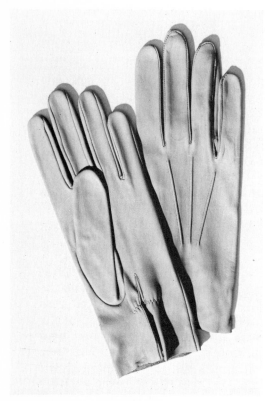

Gokey's Shooting Gloves
Courtesy Gokey Company
St. Paul, Minnesota

Game Vest
Courtesy Herter's Inc.
Waseca, Minnesota

Herter's Hudson Bay Hunting Coat
Courtesy Herter's Inc.
Waseca, Minnesota

Flotation Vest
Courtesy L.L. Bean, Inc.
Freeport, Maine

Inner Clothing

In mild weather when you're wearing a hunting coat, you need only a lightweight cotton shirt. Your normal underwear and cotton socks round out your inner clothing needs.

Footwear

Again, the type of hunting determines the footwear. Walking long distances should be done in hiking boots or foot-pacs. These also work fine in shooting out of blinds on big water.

If you're putting out decoys in shallow water, you'll need either hip boots or waders. When it's extremely warm in early fall and I'm doing lots of jump shooting, I frequently just wear tennis shoes and cotton socks. After shooting, I change into a dry pair and I'm on my way again. When you get home, throw the tennis shoes and socks in the washer-dryer and they'll be ready for morning.

Accessories

In mild weather, I wear either a camouflage hat or khaki-colored one. The main reason for wearing the hat is to reduce the exposure of your face. If your face shows up too well it will spook the birds. It's a good idea to wear a cap or hat with a visor as the visor will reduce sun glare on a bright day.

I always carry a pair of brown cotton work gloves for refurbishing blinds, etc.

WET WEATHER

Wet weather can be down right nasty! You often end up wearing clothing that restricts your movements because you need to be dry and warm.

Outer Clothing

Rain Coats — Wear a rain parka or poncho. They'll both shed the rain quite adequately. It's important to pick the right rain gear. It should be light otherwise you'll perspire and you'll be wet inside and out. Cheap raincoats sweat inside and cause condensation which will wet your interior clothing. The better rain gear, like commercial fishermen use, is the best type. I prefer not to wear a poncho-type as they restrict movement and reduce air circulation which regulates skin temperature. If you're sitting in a blind all day, poncho-types are okay; but if you're moving, get a two-piece suit.

Rain Pants — Rain pants should be light enough so that they can be tucked inside waders or hip boots. They should also not be too bulky or they'll restrict your walking. Good rain pants will keep you dry and if they have a good hard finish, they'll also allow you to walk through heavy brush without tearing.

Camouflaged Parka
Courtesy L.L. Bean, Inc.
Freeport, Maine

Camouflaged Carryall Stool. Besides sitting on, it's good for carrying extra shells, gloves, etc.
Courtesy L.L. Bean, Inc.
Freeport, Maine

*Hunting Suit
Courtesy Eddie Bauer, Inc.
Seattle, Washington*

Inner Clothing

A wool shirt will keep the upper part of your body warm. If the rain was one stage removed from snow, you might want to put the upper half of your thermal underwear on. Khaki or corduroy pants work nicely under your rain pants and the·double layer of pants will keep you warm. Your normal underwear and medium-weight socks round out your inner clothing.

Footwear

The type of shooting determines the footwear. If you're field shooting or sitting in a blind, foot-pacs or some other calf-length rubber boot is fine. Your footwear should be insulated as it's important to keep your feet warm. If it is raining hard and you're going to do quite a bit of walking, take your rain pants off and put on chest-high waders. The waders will enable you to work deeper water and also keep you dry.

Accessories

I stated earlier my preference for two-piece rain gear in which case I need a good rain hat. You should have very lightweight finger-type rubber gloves. The gloves will keep your hands dry and still give you enough sensitivity to pull the trigger when necessary. As most rain gear doesn't have a game compartment, you'll need a game vest to carry your birds, shells, etc.

CLOTHING COLORS

Colors don't necessarily spook ducks and geese but they do help the birds spot the hunter. Birds flare chiefly from movement. Obviously if something assists the birds in spotting the hunter, it's going to reduce your chances of success.

Bright colors aid the birds in spotting hunter movement. In shooting waterfowl you should stick to drab colors. On the next page we have printed a clothing analysis chart. The color chart section outlines the proper colors. Stick to the chart in your selection of waterfowl hunting clothing. Brown, olive, green, O.D., marsh colors and camouflage colors will all assist you in your hunting. Do not wear fabrics that have a sheen.

Many garment manufacturers now make clothing that have all the good qualities, warmth, lightness, mobility, as well as built-in camouflage. Stick to these and you won't go wrong.

The Chance of a lifetime. Four goose heads lined up in a row! Here you have a chance to get more than one goose with a shot.

Camouflaged Hat
Courtesy Herter's Inc.
Waseca, Minnesota

Hudson Bay Insulated Waders
Courtesy Herter's Inc.
Waseca, Minnesota

Rain Coat and Rain Pants
Courtesy Eddie Bauer, Inc.
Seattle, Washington

Clothing Analysis Chart
CONDITION

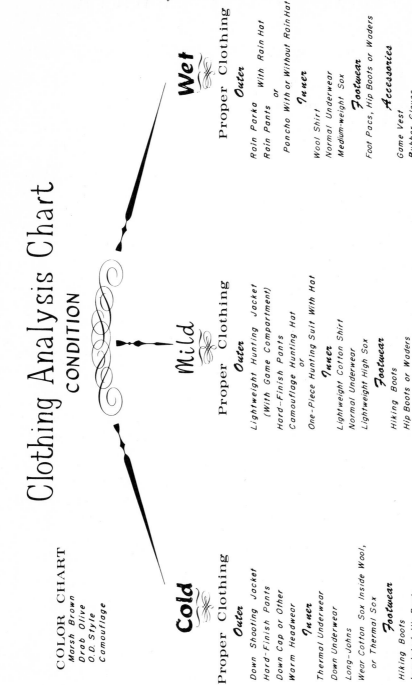

COLOR CHART
Marsh Brown
Drab Olive
O.D. Style
Camouflage

Cold

Proper Clothing

Outer
Down Shooting Jacket
Hard-Finish Pants
Down Cap or Other
Warm Headwear

Inner
Thermal Underwear
Down Underwear
Long-Johns
Wear Cotton Sox Inside Wool,
or Thermal Sox

Footwear
Hiking Boots
Insulated Hip Boots
or
Insulated Waders

Accessories
Game Vest
Shooting Gloves
Frogman Gloves

Mild

Proper Clothing

Outer
Lightweight Hunting Jacket
(With Game Compartment)
Hard-Finish Pants
Camouflage Hunting Hat
or
One-Piece Hunting Suit With Hat

Inner
Lightweight Cotton Shirt
Normal Underwear
Lightweight High Sox

Footwear
Hiking Boots
Hip Boots or Waders

Accessories
Brown Cotton Gloves

Wet

Proper Clothing

Outer
Rain Parka   With Rain Hat
Rain Pants
or
Poncho With or Without Rain Hat

Inner
Wool Shirt
Normal Underwear
Medium-weight Sox

Footwear
Foot Pacs, Hip Boots or Waders

Accessories
Game Vest
Rubber Gloves

Chapter 22
MIRTH IN THE MARSHES

This is a collection of faux pas, "witties" and a few poems that we have found amusing while going down life's trail.

"Jack and the Cornstalk"

Several years ago, two individuals joined our duck club. Jovial characters, they were always doing something to make life a little more pleasant. Several seasons ago they had come by a huge supply of corn which was part of their business. They decided, in one of their generous moods, to donate several sacks of corn to the club.

We decided, as it was several weeks before hunting season opened, to accept their generous offer. Thousands of ducks and geese responded to our corn donation. But they had every last kernel cleaned up two weeks before hunting season opened.

Very close to our property there is a town called Odessa. In it lived several characters who resented the amount of birds using our area. They decided to have a little fun and went out and bought some corn. They saved the corn until about three days before hunting season opened, then scattered it along the edges of the lake. The birds again responded. The town "villains" called the game wardens who kept an "eye" on the lake. The birds cleaned up 99 and 44/100's of the corn but there was still a little left, not noticeable to the naked eye.

Opening day came bright and sunny; however, by nightfall things weren't too funny. When the first shot was fired exactly at high noon, a team of wardens swooped down on us and six individuals were arrested. We, of course, protested our innocence but to no avail.

One of the arrested members, who we'll call "Jack," had to leave for home. Two of the other members decided to have a little fun at "Jack's" expense. They sent a limerick telegram to "Jack's" wife which they had the gall to charge to my phone number. It read:

There were some guys from Odessa
Who got Paul and his friends in a messa.
They scattered the corn,
And the cops blew the horn,
Where they are now, you can guessa.

The "Gay" Duck Club

A group of "odd fellows" had gotten together and formed a duck club. Despite their femininity, they were pretty good hunters. They built some good blinds and posted the property. However, their signs weren't too motivating as all they said was "Keep Out." They were overrun with poachers.

179

They finally had a directors meeting and decided to resolve the problem — debut a new sign! The sign read:

No Hunting
Trespassers Will be Violated

Almost immediately, poaching fell off to nothing.

A Goose in Hand

I once told one of our older members, "A goose in hand is worth two in the bush." Little did I know how that comment would come back to haunt me. Several seasons went by; then one morning we spotted 10,000 geese feeding in a meadow that had a small pothole adjacent to it.

I instructed the oldtimer and his two companions to go south around the pothole and hide in the draw. As the wind was blowing east to west, I knew the birds would take off with the prevailing wind and go right over them. They took off and I started leisurely picking my way through the sagebrush, keeping enough cover between me and the geese so that I wouldn't be seen. I had advanced to within seventy-five yards of the geese. Suddenly I heard some loud gabbling. Something was bothering the geese and they were getting quite nervous. I figured a coyote or something had spooked them. I sat down and the birds began to feed again.

For no apparent reason, seven geese got up and flew south. They were only ten yards high at the most. A thought occurred to me. Those birds were headed right for my friends. The clear morning air was shattered by several shots. The entire mass of geese got up and flew west, totally unscathed. I couldn't believe my eyes!

In a few moments the three stalkers appeared. My friend with the white beard proudly exclaimed, "Well, Paul, I got one!", as he grinned from ear to ear. I didn't have the heart to say anything but I thought about the 9,999 survivors without pleasure.

The Free Ride

Several of us were shooting ducks one evening in a local swamp. Shooting had been very good and we were about "limited out." Only Bob was "light" and he needed one more bird.

Somebody yelled "mark" and I noticed several nice Mallards tooling around. We gave them a couple of toots on the old call. They cupped their wings and began their descent. Bob picked a nice fat Greenhead and crumpled it with his first shot. One of the other boys who was closest to the bird picked it up and commented that the bird didn't have a mark on it.

We laughed a little and told Bob he probably scared the bird to death. We ambled back to the station wagon, put the guns and birds in and proceeded to have a martini. After finishing our martinis, we drove back toward the motel which was about ten miles away. We pulled up in front of the room and Bob ran the electric window down. We started to unload our gear when there was a great "woosh."

Bob's "no mark" mallard made the prettiest launch you ever saw. When last seen the Mallard was flying over the Cimarron Motel saying to himself, "Hmmm, ten miles and I never beat a wing."

The Duck Calling Dude

Several years ago at the start of one of our preseason duck calling classes, we were mentally sizing up the participants. There was one rather nattily attired gentleman who presented a striking appearance. Tall, good-looking, with shocks of steel-gray hair, he looked the part of the sophisticated hunter. He looked so knowledgeable, it was almost questionable as to why he was even there.

We started the class and had made it through the fundamentals. We started discussing the "alarm sound." The stately gentleman raised his hand and asked if we would demonstrate the "alarm sound." As we started to call, his face suddenly became quite flushed and he slammed his fist down on the table and shouted, "Damn, that was my best call!"

Laughing Strikes Twice

Several of our duck calling classes had been filmed for regional television shows. On the filming of one of these shows, as the crew was setting up their equipment, we noticed one class member looking a little ill.

We inquired if he was getting stage fright or was he actually sick. With a pained expression, he told his story: "Last year I was watching this outdoor TV show and a bunch of guys came running out on stage making this tremendous racket — babbling duck calls all over the place. I just cracked up and rolled on the floor and laughed so hard I lost my breath.

"I couldn't believe anyone could be so foolish. Now here I am about to do the same thing. I can just see all those people out there holding their sides and laughing at me! Well, I think I'm going to be sick."

A Titter About Litter

November 7, 1969

Mr. Herb Quinn
1000 Ivy
Moses Lake, Washington   98837

Re: Your activity at Mud Rock Bird Watching Area

Dear Mr. Quinn:

On a recent trip to the Mud Rock Goose Watching Area, I had occasion to shoot in the North Blind. It seems that every time a flock of geese came by they were spooked. There was no apparent reason for their behavior. At long last a great olde gander (wise) came by leading a flock of other geese.

He came close enough for me to shoot at. I winged him and he sailed about a half mile away. I went over to dispatch him and he said:

"Man, you've got a bad scene going. If I give you some good advice, will you spare my life?"

I replied I would and he said:

"The main reason the geese are spooking when they go by your blind is that you have some problem with litterbugs. If the blinds were well policed, you would then again have good goose shooting."

I thanked him and he flew off into the sunset towards Tatoosh Island.

I then returned to the blind and upon examining the outside of it, found a few assorted goodies, i.e., steelhead punch card, Shriner's card, last year's deer tag, etc., which I am returning to you forthwith since they may be of some value to you.

Based on the olde gander's comments, I feel that appropriate use of the enclosure will considerably aid the Mud Rock Goose Shooting Area.

However, consistent with the national trend, you are afforded the opportunity to protest. You and your employees may stage a protest rally at the Mud Rock West Gate at 6:30 a.m. on Wednesday next. As long as your demonstration is not too loud, we will allow it.

Sincerely,

Paul S. Bernsen, President
Mud Rock Anti-litter Corps

PSB:pcd
Enclosures
P.S. We hope you use this camouflaged wastebasket to good advantage!

Under Warranty?

October 28, 1970

Mr. Harry B. Dye
Dye-Call Company
1309 North 77th Street
Seattle, Washington

Dear Harry:

Enclosed is what remains of the duck call belonging to Donald Miller, Mayor of Enumclaw, Washington.

It seems that Mr. Miller was in the wasteland of Eastern Washington attempting to get a return on his investment in your duck calling classes and it became necessary to discipline his Labrador. While he was beating the animal about the head and shoulders he discovered he had neglected to remove the duck call from his hand. Needless to say, when the call and the Lab's head came in contact with each other the rigidity of the Lab won out and parts of the call were scattered over a large portion of Section 5.

We are sure that a man of your experience would have designed your duck calls to withstand the rigors of hunting as well as any stresses involved while beating a dog. Mayor Miller therefore, feels it should be repaired under warranty. If not please feel free to bill us in an amount you feel appropriate.

Sincerely,

J.E. Warren

JEW:ab

Dude Watching

Anyone who claims to be a waterfowl hunter is driven by a special force known only to himself, whether it be struggling out of a warm bed in anticipation of shooting a limit or just getting up to sit in a duck blind to enjoy a few hours away from the routine of every other morning. The important thing is that the morning progresses in a manner somewhat as that expected. With one or another of these motivations in mind, we left Seattle Friday afternoon. Our car resounded with the din and roar of goose and duck calls as we chided each other about our individual lack of technique. The 180-mile drive to Othello passed quickly, as would be the case with good company and heightening spirits anticipating the next morning's hunt.

This particular weekend was a little unusual as I had agreed to "guide" some dudes for "Potholes Paul" who has a duck club in Eastern Washington. Potholes had entrusted me with getting three couples to their blind assignments for that weekend. Potholes had abandoned duck hunting in favor of watching Sonny Sixkiller throw T.D. passes as he had been "dude watching" for six straight weeks. I volunteered to guide for him. I had looked forward to it with considerable anticipation, for I knew all but one area in our hunting domain well, and could provide my group with capable, even professional, guide services.

At 8:30 p.m. we met with our weekend coordinator to find out what area we were to hunt, and who my two companions and I would be guiding. Our assigned areas, called "Canyon Lake" and "Moonshot" were located two miles apart, nearly in the middle of the block of land I was least familiar with. I had worked in the area for part of a day, but had never hunted there. To this thought, our coordinator replied that Tony, one of the other guides, would be going and had hunted there. He also drew a road map on the rumpled paper napkin before him, then told us to be at the resturant at 4:30 a.m. With that, we went to our motel room.

At 4:30 a.m. our respective groups assembled, had breakfast, and headed for our areas. There was some confusion about the first turn off the highway. The map drawn the night before indicated road E-18, but Tony corrected that to E-20. Our group of three vehicles turned into the vast sage-strewn Moteet Springs tract. We had gone several miles when the road divided, then deadended in a swamp. Everyone got re-directed to the road division. We reassured our three husband and wife teams that all was in

183

control. From this point forward things deteriorated rapidly. Several more times we assured our three couples that all was in control, but as the first rays of sunrise began to show, the credibility gap between guide and "dude" widened. No longer were the faces in the two station wagons friendly. Finally, we found Moonshot we thought. We left Mr. and Mrs. K and Tony, then headed for Canyon Lake. Wrong road again. Good God — what an empty feeling. I decided we had to admit what our remaining two couples already knew. *Their guide was lost!* My two companions attempted to lessen my utter self-disgust without success. Vern had driven his Wagoneer over and through terrain no vehicle should be subjected to, and Bob sprinted through water and scaled hills looking for lakes in the distance. Worst of all, for our three couples, I had destroyed all the exciting thoughts duck hunters have the night before a hunt. To make matters worse, when we did find Canyon Lake, long after sunrise, it was carpeted with several thousand mallards.

We returned to our noon meeting with the coordinator. Tony was already there and had recounted most of our morning's disaster. The coordinator said only a few "dudes" planned to attend the evening shoot, so my guiding career ended. Bob, Vern and I decided to have lunch with cocktails, take a nap in the now warm sun and maybe hunt ourselves in the evening.

About two hours later, we were awakened by the coordinator who said our two couples from the morning wanted to shoot, and for some reason accepted me as their guide. I was to take them to the "Deep Dark Swamp," an area I knew well. Bob and Vern were to hunt at a different area. At this point my self esteem was beginning to return somewhat because Mr. and Mrs. A and Mr. and Mrs. M were giving me one more chance. We drove a short distance to the Swamp and got ready. Fortunately, the mallards did not let me down, for we had 30 minutes of fast shooting as hunting hours ended. The five of us returned to the car with two limits of mallards between us and headed back to the motel.

I was sitting in the middle of the front seat beginning to warm up from the nip in the evening air. The car heater was just right, and my bulging jacket was extra-comfortable. By now, I was thinking what a nice day it turned out to be after all. I must have been napping when Mrs. A's voice from the back seat asked, "Who in this car has had a cocktail?" In turn, each of my wards replied, "Not I." Instantly my pleasant thoughts of moments before shattered as that gravelly and unfamiliar voice replied, "I did." I was the last of the five hunters in the car to respond to Mrs. A's question. That horrible surge of panic overwhelmed my throat just as I said, "I did." The resulting voice was gravelly and unfamiliar. In the following ten minutes not one word was spoken. I do not recall exhaling the entire time, but then it would have taken a divine act to have caused me to exhale again.

As I turned into the motel and dropped each of the "dudes" off, I thought of "Potholes" and his football game and what he'd say when he got back from Seattle. Much to my surprise he didn't say a thing. But several weeks later at the annual duck club dinner, he shook my hand as he presented me with the "Lief Erickson Explorer Award." When I got back to my table, I opened my award which was a pair of $1.98 binoculars and a map of the area we'd been lost in. There was also a thank you card. It said, "For Dude Watching" and was signed by "Potholes Paul."

THE HUMOR AND TRUTH ABOUT DUCK HUNTING

The hunters of ducks are a crazy breed—
A hole in the mud is all they need —
A place to hide from flying duck —
In eighty acres of smelly muck.
The roads are bumpy — in rain, they walk
But the dumb duck hunter will never squawk.
Tho' he slips in mud and wets his butt,
He won't complain, 'cause he's a nut!
If it were not so, he'd stay with his wife
And give his children a chance in life,
Instead of cavorting around, by heck--
And becoming a useless swivel-neck.
The hike from the car to the beat-up blind
Would make an elephant sore behind.
They wade in slime that would bog a flea
Like a bunch of bums with housemaid's knee!
They stagger and stumble and sweat and swear
When the flashlight shows they're half-way there.
They gasp for breath and their muscles crack,
They hope they won't have a heart attack.
THEN THE MUD-HENS CACKLE, THE MALLARDS FLARE, AND THE
        HUNTERS PRANCE LIKE FRED ASTAIRE.
They fling decoys from sodden sacks,
And ninety percent land on their backs.
Then they stumble back and fall in the hole
With a crick in the back, but joy in the soul.
There they wait for dawn, all cramped and grim,
Hoping to hell the ducks come in.
Their eyes burn out in the mid-day glare,
And duck lice delve in their thinning hair.
They hunt for cripples with a galloping tread
And get back to the blind so nearly dead
That their duck calls sound like a weak Bronx cheer,
And the ducks get the Hell right out of "here."
I say it's wicked for a man with a brain
To risk his life in fog and rain,
To wreck his muscles and damn his soul
Just to squat in the mud of a slimy hole.
Would I ruin my health and risk my life
And get in bad with the little wife,
Just to sit in a blind and suffer pain
In snow and wind and sleeting rain?
Would I spend my money and waste my time,
And listen to lies in the winter time?
Would I do these things no sane man should?
BROTHER, YOU'RE RIGHT, I WOULD.

COMPLIMENTS OF THE WASHINGTON DUCK HUNTERS

The Minneapolis Star

Sports

Tuesday, April 18, 1972

DUCK HUNTING IN 1975?
HERE ARE THE 'FACTS'!

By Charles Johnson — Lowdown on Sports

What will duck hunting be like in 1975?

Even the scientists, biologists and other experts wouldn't hazard a guess at this time.

But an anonymous author with a sense of humor offers his thoughts in a letter that apparently is getting good circulation these days.

Because the "forecast" of regulations in 1975 furnishes many good laughs, we thought we should pass them on to frustrated hunters.

Don't blame us for this outburst. Don't take it seriously. Might save it until 1975 to see how far off the author back in 1972 really was.

Anyway, here are "likely 1975 regulations."

"OPENING — Oct. 2, at 10:14 a.m.

"CLOSING — Oct. 16, at 8:17.6 a.m.

"Shooting will be allowed from 10:14 a.m. until noon on every other day during the season provided the wind velocity does not exceed 4.5 miles per hour.

LIMITS

"Bag limits are simplified this year. Two female Coots may be taken or one male Coot and one female Sawbill. Hunters who have not taken one day's limit as explained above and after making a sworn statement to that effect in federal court, may apply for the Audubon Permit to kill one four-year-old Spoonbill. Hunters will be notified when the Spoonbill quota is reached in each principal flyway.

"Due to the increase in Mallard ducks in Ontario, Alberta, Manitoba and Saskatchewan, one Mallard duck may be killed on the third day of the season, but hunters must not kill Ontario Mallards. All Ontario Mallards have slightly jaundiced eyeballs which are readily observable by watchful hunters. When a legal Mallard is bagged, it must be taken immediately to the capitol of the state it was shot in, for proper identification by conservation crews, who will also supply the picking and cleaning permit ($2).

BLINDS AND CLOTHING

"A blind will consist of three branches from local trees or bushes and may be no larger than the hunter's thumb at the first joint. Club blinds, where hunters rotate between blinds, must use the thumb of the smallest member for the measurement of all blinds. Blinds must be 41.8 yards from the nearest vegetation. As in recent years, all wearing apparel (boots, pants, coat, gloves, etc.) must be either highway yellow or stop-light red in color. The official government 'Keep 'em Flying' cap with the battery operated blinker light on the bill is mandatory and may be purchased at any post office.

"Hunters are warned that game wardens may search their persons for the mandatory three spare batteries. This measure is necessary in light of the many dead batteries used as excuses last year.

GUNS AND AMMUNITION

"All gauges of shotgun may be used up to and including 28 gauge, any barrel length. Stocks, however, may not exceed six inches in length, regardless of hunter's arm length.

CALLING REGULATIONS

"Manufactured duck calls, mouth actuated, are illegal again this year due to the high degree of proficiency attained by a number of hunters in imitating ducks by voice alone. It is now necessary to place minor restrictions on the activity of voice calling. Any hunter (or guide) who shall endeavor to attract wildfowl by emitting misleading sounds by mouth, must hold in his oral cavity not less than two one-inch ball bearings while doing so.

"To avoid hardship to the hunter, should either or both ball bearings be swallowed during the shoot, continued calling by mouth will be considered legal if each imitating utterance is followed by the cry 'Powder River,' uttered with the same degree of sound and intensity."

Any person wearing dentures, partial plates or bridges in public hunting areas must leave them with the game warden assigned to that area. The U.S. Fish and Wildlife Service has ruled that persons wearing such dental devices have achieved a proficient feeding chuckle by rolling the ball bearings against the ends of such devices. As feeding chuckles have been illegal for three years, they have become alarmed at the increased amount of full-mouth tooth extractions which avid hunters have been getting. Private gun club members must leave their dental devices in the glove compartment of their cars. This regulation could, however, be rescinded by opening day as various dental societies have vigorous lobbying going on in Washington protesting this unfair ruling.

HUNTER, WARDEN REGULATIONS

"Remember that the warden is your friend! This year to further promote this fact, you need not address state game wardens as, 'Your Majesty.' Only the federal wardens are addressed as such. You will, of course, share your refreshments with these jolly fellows so that they may, in a more congenial atmosphere, check your license, stamp, permits, citizenship papers, bank account, fingerprints, church affiliation, racial extraction, political connections and I.Q.

IN CONCLUSION . . .

"We hope that all the more fortunate hunters who have been lucky to provide themselves with a place to shoot, will co-operate with the department's program, 'Open your land to the public.' Remember, the number of strangers you allow to hunt on your marshes will determine how long we refrain from draining it."

Chapter 23
MY FAVORITE RECIPES

Much has been said about the "game of wild cooking" and not enough has been said about the "cooking of wild game." Poorly cooked game probably has been the basis for more family arguments and turned up noses than any other phase of family food consumption. Properly prepared, nothing compares with the wonderful flavors and tastes of duck, geese and pheasant.

In order to partake of these epicurean delights, there are a few preliminary steps that must be taken:

1. When game is shot, the sooner the body temperature can be reduced the better. In early fall when the weather is warmer, get the birds in some shade. Hang your duck stringer over the limb of a tree. If there is no natural shade available, open your car trunk and leave the lid up so that air can circulate.

2. Never pile birds up! The ones at the bottom can spoil from the body temperature of the others. Spread them out so they can cool.

3. If your hunting trip is going to be extended, the birds should be field-dressed (entrails removed).

4. Get them to your "duck plucker" as soon as possible. If you don't know one, look in the yellow pages of your phone book under Poultry Processors. This is usually where a "plucker" will turn up.

Now that we have an oven-ready product, we can begin our culinary adventures.

Ducks and How to Prepare Them

Prime Mallard or any other large duck should be treated with the same high regard you have for a piece of prime steer. In other words, if you are accustomed to eating beef rare, medium-rare or well-done, you should give the duck the same opportunity. Over cooking results in a tough, dry, flavorless bird! They should not be cooked too long!

Roast Western Style Mallard

As most of the meat is located on the breast and legs you'll need one Mallard per person. After rinsing the cavity and exterior, brush each bird liberally with melted butter or margarine. Sprinkle the birds lightly with salt and pepper. Place them breast side up in a roasting pan. Put the roasting pan in the refrigerator which allows the butter to congeal. Five minutes is adequate. Allowing the butter to congeal will aid the browning process as the bird is roasting. Turn your oven to 500°. For rare duck, leave your oven at 500° for 12 minutes, then 325° for 6 minutes. For medium-rare duck — 500° for 15 minutes, 325° for 6 minutes. For well-done duck — 500° for 20 minutes, 325° for 12 minutes. The intense heat of 500° in a preheated oven sears the meat, locking in all the juices.

When cooking ducks rare, only the breasts and legs will be tender. I suggest you use the remainder of the bird for soup stock as outlined in my "Wild Duck Soup" recipe which appears later in this chapter.

Wild Duck Ala Mushroom Sauce

Remove breasts and legs from six large ducks. Roll pieces of duck in flour or Bisquick very liberally. Place skin side down in preheated electric frypan (375°). Oil should be 1/4-inch deep in frypan. When both sides are nicely browned, remove to platter. Dry each piece individually with paper towel. Pour oil from pan. Add 2 cans of mushroom soup and 2 cans water. Stir mixture as necessary to boiling level. Add duck and simmer for 1½ hours. Mushroom stock becomes the gravy base. Remove duck and add water if necessary to liquid to allow mixture smoothness. Bring gravy to boil and serve with whipped potatoes or wild rice. Serves ten.

Roast Honker

Older geese run a little to the tough side. You can determine their age by their size. A twelve to thirteen-pound goose is a very mature bird. Seven to nine-pound birds are ideal.

To prepare, rinse bird thoroughly inside·and out. Salt and pepper, including cavity. Baste exterior of bird with melted butter or margarine. Place bird in refrigerator until butter has congealed. Remove bird, place in shallow roasting pan. Place bird in preheated 450° oven. Roast for 30 minutes. Remove bird and stuff with our Roast Duck Stuffing or your favorite stuffing. Reduce heat to 325°. When bird is golden brown cover with aluminum foil. Allow approximately 2¾ hours from time of stuffing. Periodically add water to roasting pan, as the steam will help tenderize the bird.

Wild Duck Soup

Take duck carcasses (at least two) and place in large pot with 8 cups of boiling water. Add 1 teaspoon of seasoning salt. Bring to boil. Cook 20 minutes. Take carcasses from pot, remove meat and place everything back in pot. Add: 2 cups cubed duck breasts (3/4-inch cubes), 1 cup chopped celery, 1 cup diced onion, and salt and pepper to taste. Cover entire mixture with water. Bring to boil, turn to medium heat, cook for 1 hour. Add 2 cups diced potatoes and cook for 1 hour more. If stock becomes too thick add modest amount of water. When soup is done remove carcasses and serve. Excellent with french bread.

Roast Duck Stuffing

We use stuffing that is fully cooked. The bird-cooking process is the same as described in our "Western Style Mallard" recipe.

Melt 1 cube butter or margarine in electric frying pan. Add 1/4 cup chopped onion. When onion is lightly browned, add 2½ cups hot water, 3 cups cooked wild rice, 1 tablespoon minced parsley, 5 chicken bouillon cubes and 1 cup coarsely chopped walnuts. Bring mixture to boil for 15 minutes. Reduce heat to simmer and simmer for 20 minutes, adding moisture as necessary. After cooking period sprinkle lightly with salt and pepper and stuff each bird. Recipe will stuff four birds.

If all the participants are of the well-done school, the birds should be covered with aluminum foil after they are browned. During roasting add water to the bottom of the pan so that the birds will stay moist.

Breast of Canada Goose with Mushroom Wine Sauce

Remove breasts and legs from three geese. Salt and pepper and flour pieces. Place skin side down in preheated electric frypan 375°. Use 1/4 inch Planters Peanut oil for cooking oil. When both sides are nicely browned, remove and drain on paper towel.

Pour oil from pan, saving drippings, add two cans Campbell's Golden Mushroom soup, 2 cans water, and 1/3 bottle Tawny Port wine. Bring liquid to boil, cook at 275° in covered frypan for 1½ hours. Add equal parts of wine and water as necessary which will insure a smooth gravy. Serves ten.

Orange Mallard

Definitely the way for those who like well-done duck and a pleasant change for those who are used to eating duck rare.

Take two Mallards, rinse inside and out. Salt and pepper cavity. Place in roasting pan, breast up. Baste birds completely with the following marinade:

1/2 cup sugar
1/2 cup soy sauce
1 orange peel, grated
1 ounce thinly sliced fresh ginger
2 cloves crushed garlic
1/3 cup red wine
dash monosodium glutamate

Mix marinade thoroughly, baste birds occasionally while cooking with the marinade. Cook birds 300° for 2 hours covered and 1 hour uncovered.

A hearty thank you to Paul and Virginia Hirai, Moses Lake, Washington.

Sweet and Sour Goose

Cut 6 pounds of goose (or duck) into 1-inch squares. Allow meat to marinate for two hours in the following mixture:

3 ounces bourbon
4 cloves garlic, crushed or chopped very fine
1¼ cups soy sauce
2 Tablespoons sugar
2 Teaspoons Kitchen Bouquet

After marinating, drain meat, and flour as you would fried chicken. Cook in deep fat at 350° for 6 minutes, stirring occasionally. Pour sweet and sour sauce over meat. Garnish with candied ginger and scallions if desired.

Sweet and Sour Sauce:

1 quart pork broth
1¾ cups brown sugar
1 cup vinegar
1 ounce chunk fresh ginger, crushed
    (remove chunk when sauce is done)

Blend the pork broth, brown sugar and vinegar; add crushed chunk of ginger. Bring mixture to a boil and simmer for 15 minutes. Return to vigorous boil and thicken with cornstarch for consistency. Add Kitchen Bouquet for color.

A tip of the hat to Mr. Jack Eng, owner of Elmer's Restaurant, Moses Lake, Washington.

Conclusion
THE FUTURE OF
WATERFOWL HUNTING

To look at the future of waterfowl hunting in the proper perspective let's first examine the past. If it wasn't for the eye-opening thirties, our past seasons would have been very poor. Instead of increased bag limits, broader shooting frameworks in most flyways, and the easing of restrictions on birds like the Canvasback, Redhead and Wood Duck, we might all be spending each fall looking at waterfowl paintings instead of the actual birds.

Why were the late sixties good when the thirties looked so bleak and why will the seventies be better than the sixties? *Because* somebody did something — that's why! When people do something, results occur. Action properly harnessed produces benefits. According to human behavior studies, motivation produces action, but only two things produce motivation — a loss or a gain.

The threat of a loss was the motivation that stirred a few dedicated people in 1929. The possible loss of one of our most valued natural resources — waterfowl. It moved these sportsmen to such an extent that *they did something*! Their actions were the spawning grounds for Ducks Unlimited.

This dedicated group of sportsmen created an organization called "More Game Birds In America Foundation." They founded it because it had become believable that waterfowling was on the brink of becoming a memory. Civilization had rapidly sprawled westward across the North American Continent, like a hugh wave encompassing the prairie areas of both Canada and the United States. Among sportsmen-conservationists there soon arose a disturbing observation — the vast, sky-darkening flocks of ducks were rapidly disappearing. As the waterfowl populations continued their downward plunge toward oblivion, the concern mounted into full-scale alarm giving rise to dire predictions of the death of our waterfowling heritage.

In this darkest hour, the solid foundation of Ducks Unlimited was formed. The members of "More Game Birds In America Foundation" set out to search for the answers to the dismal problems responsible for the tragic decrease of continental waterfowl populations. The foundation launched an intensive study lasting several years. Among the survey's conclusions: (1) over 65 percent of the continent's waterfowl begin life in the three rich Canadian Prairie Provinces of Alberta, Saskatchewan and Manitoba; (2) the irresistible onslaught of civilization, through draining and cultivation, was steadily ravishing the prime breeding grounds; (3) natural droughts and floods were becoming increasingly critical as a limiting factor in waterfowl production. Finally, the study concluded that if the duck and goose populations were to be maintained and restored, then immediate efforts must begin in the gigantic task of rehabilitating and preserving the primary nesting areas of Canada.

Ducks Unlimited Is Born

To attack this monumental task, a group of farsighted American sportsmen banded together to form Ducks Unlimited. It was January 29, 1937, that DU was incorporated in the Nation's capitol as a unique nonprofit membership organization, dedicated to the wise conservation of waterfowl and the perpetuation of the noble heritage of waterfowling.

The U.S. Government, realizing that federal funds could not be spent for conservation in Canada (even though American sportsmen gained primary benefit), granted tax exemption for contributions to DU's ambitious programs of reclaiming and preserving the prime waterfowl breeding grounds. To actually construct the projects, and to handle the many facets of such a gigantic building program, a companion Canadian corporation called Ducks Unlimited (Canada) was formed, under laws of the Dominion.

Needless to say, DU was sternly faced with problems of immense proportion when dirt was turned on its first wetlands project, Manitoba's Big Grass Marsh, in 1938. Even though a serious depression lingered in both the U.S. and Canada, the determined outdoorsmen pulled up their boots and waded in. To the wholehearted support of American sportsmen was added the invaluable cooperation of Canada's Provincial and Dominion governments, plus that of ranchers, landholders, communities and industries, who generously granted no-cost, long-term land leases on wetland areas.

The result — a program of truly international cooperation in conservation, is a brotherhood that has been unrivaled anywhere. The noble cause of Ducks Unlimited — pioneering in the wise conservation of North America's valuable waterfowl resources — has, from the very beginning, been championed by sportsmen who have made the future of our ducks and geese the concern of all, from the highest government agency to the "one-gallused" hunter.

Thirty-five Years of Pioneering

Since this extraordinary conservation movement was initiated three-and-a-half decades ago, Ducks Unlimited has led the way in the perpetuation of waterfowl, utilizing all facilities at its command to restore, preserve and create nesting habitat for ducks and geese. Ducks Unlimited has expended over $19 million to plan, build and develop well over 1,000 duck "factories," as its projects are appropriately called by sportsmen and wildlife officials. All told, since work first began in 1938, over 1,200 water control structures, such as dams, dikes and levies, have been constructed. Today, Ducks Unlimited has, under lease, over two million acres of prime wetland habitat, with total shoreline (a vital ingredient of top-quality production) measuring over 9,000 miles.

DU's water control projects range from valuable small units of less than fifty acres to hugh marshland complexes of over half a million acres in area. Construction is currently in high gear on one of the largest and most ambitious programs ever tackled — the 512,000-acre Mawdesley Wildlife Development, called the Del-Mar Project, near the Pas in Manitoba.

It is the moral obligation of today's sportsman to assure future generations that their skies will never be empty!
Courtesy Ducks Unlimited

While the majority of projects are built in the rich Prairie Provinces of Manitoba, Saskatchewan and Alberta, Ducks Unlimited production units stretch across Canada, from the Serpentine River Flats Project in southwest British Columbia to the prime 6,000-acre Delaware State Project at Missaquash Marsh, on the border between Nova Scotia and New Brunswick.

Many of DU's project units have been named to honor conservation leaders while others, financed by sportsmen and DU committees, bear the names of states, cities and individuals. Across the breadth of the Dominion, these 'Donor Lake" projects are readily identified by sturdy commemorative cairns, bearing bronze plaques noting the names of donors.

In conjunction with the wide-ranging construction programs, hundreds of miles of fencing have been erected to protect nesting areas; many miles of fire lanes are maintained to thwart devastating marsh fires. DU (Canada)'s highly trained biologists and engineers regularly inspect projects, evaluating production, supervising planting of aquatic food plants and directing the numerous other tasks essential to insuring top utilization of the areas. Field crews have banded over 160,000 ducks and geese as part of the continuing wildfowl research studies.

During early 1970, Ducks Unlimited's programs became truly continental in scope, with the launching of Ducks Unlimited de Mexico. The new organization, composed of Mexican sportsmen, is raising funds within that nation, which will be dedicated to waterfowl conservation and management programs in Mexico.

Over the thirty-five years of its progressive achievement, Ducks Unlimited has raised a total of well over $25 million in contributions from concerned sportsmen and organizations in the U.S. and Canada. Needless to say, DU is justly proud of the fact that, since its founding, almost $.80 of every dollar has gone directly to Canada to be judiciously spent in the never-ending battle to preserve, protect and restore the vital waterfowl breeding grounds.

Ducks Unlimited and You

The distinguished record compiled by Ducks Unlimited over the years stands as a concrete tribute to the unselfish efforts of the devoted sportsmen-conservationists who, in reality, are DU. Among its officers and trustees, now and over past years, are leaders in business, industry, the professions and, most of all, conservation. While serving without compensation, their full satisfaction comes in the vital role they play in preserving your precious waterfowl inheritance. Well over 70,000 persons are members of DU, yet millions enjoy the benefits of this valuable natural resource. Every hunter who treasures his sport, and every person who shares the thrills of watching waterfowl, owes a real vote of gratitude to those who have borne the responsibilities of helping perpetuate the continent's ducks and geese.

A look at Ducks Unlimited's outstanding chronicle of conservation achievement makes it easy to understand the· great pride each Ducks Unlimited member takes in his association. This progressive record is most certainly deserving of full support from every conservation- concerned American.

Before Ducks Unlimited: a dusty, dried-up lake bed thirty miles southwest of Brooks, Alberta, Canada.
Courtesy Ducks Unlimited

After Ducks Unlimited: eighty-seven acres of prime waterfowl habitat with 3.8 miles of shoreline — loaded, year after year, with growing ducks.
Courtesy Ducks Unlimited

DU has clearly illustrated that the rehabilitation of prime nesting grounds across Canada is a vital factor in the preservation of our waterfowl — and in the process has achieved the equally important goal of instilling a solid awareness, among citizens and government agencies alike on both sides of the border, of the urgent need for wise conservation programs.

Facing the Future

With the return of abundant water to the primary breeding regions, Ducks Unlimited is faced with a highly unusual opportunity and challenge. Forging ahead with an aggressive program of project construction now will provide and protect much valuable habitat from future floods and drought.

Ducks Unlimited, in cooperation with government agencies and landowners, has activated a new "master plan for the 70's," calling for turning an additional 4,500,000 acres of Canadian waterfowl habitat into "drought-proof" duck factories by 1980 — a mighty big job! In fact, one which will require DU to raise at least 20 percent more each succeeding year.

The funds which are so necessary to accomplish this long-range goal must, in large part, come from here in the United States, where sportsmen realize almost 75 percent of the continental waterfowl harvest. American outdoorsmen are not prone to sidestep their responsibilities in matters involving conservation, as witnessed by longtime support of DU and other worthy programs designed to protect natural resources. Several states have passed legislation setting aside a portion of hunting license fees for waterfowl conservation and, noting DU's fine record for making every donated dollar count, have granted these funds to Ducks Unlimited. There is bright optimism that several other states may follow in the progressive footsteps of such states as Louisiana, Ohio, North Carolina, Wisconsin, Tennessee, Arkansas, Pennsylvania and South Carolina. There is also confidence that sportsmen of the U.S. and Canada will continue to recognize the critical need for their support of Ducks Unlimited's every expanding efforts.

Through generous contributions of time, service and money to their local and state committees, DU members are doing their part in enlarging their own memorable enjoyment of a day in their favorite marsh, while at the same time aiding the preservation of our priceless waterfowl heritage for their sons and grandsons to follow.

"THE WISE CONSERVATION OF OUR WATERFOWL IS THE RESPONSIBILITY AND OBLIGATION OF ALL WHO THRILL TO THE SIGHT AND SOUND OF THESE NOBLE CREATURES."

What You Can Do

The Ducks Unlimited quotation you have just read truly exemplifies the goals and purposes of Ducks Unlimited. As in the past and present, with a helping hand from you and other sportsmen-conservationists, the noble and remarkable accomplishments of Ducks Unlimited will continue into the unlimited future.

Ducks Unlimited needs you and you need Ducks Unlimited. Your time has come to "take a turn at the duck factory." You can help in two ways. One, by making a tax deductible donation, and the other, by giving of yourself. Join your nearest DU chapter and "take a turn"! Go out and encourage a few nonshooters to make a donation. The nonshooters in the U.S. and Canada total ten million interested bird watchers. These ten million bird watchers are all around you — trappers, fishermen, ornithologists, teachers, artists, wood carvers and nature lovers to name just a few. They'd shoulder part of the burden if you asked.

Everyone derives some benefits out of DU's work. But most important, other endangered species of birds and animals have been assisted in their battle for survival. All forms of life need water, and the benefits of DU projects in Canada have been extended to 251 species of birds, 60 different mammals and 10 types of fish. For farmers and cattlemen, additional irrigation water, flood control and superior grazing have all been fringe benefits in their cooperation with DU.

Ducks Unlimited gets maximum mileage out of their dollar. They *buy no land*! Project areas are provided DU by the Canadian government under a free easement agreement which runs for twenty-one years with an option to renew. On private lands, their project usage runs in perpetuity.

There are 2,500,000 waterfowlers in the U.S. and Canada. If you add this to the known bird watchers, it adds up to 12,500,000 people who are interested in the future of waterfowl. There are 70,000 members of Ducks Unlimited. It would appear that less than 1% of the total amount of interested people are supporting the interests of the other 99%. I think that you'll agree that we need a bigger percent of participation. Let's *all* get together and turn "wasteland into wetland." There's an application and a self-addressed envelope in this book. Get motivated — *you* have something to gain!

*Aerial view of camp and inlet control for Ohio lakes.
Courtesy Ducks Unlimited*

*Dragline work on Del-Mar Project produces results like this:
Courtesy Ducks Unlimited*

A New "Duck Factory" — This is Ducks Unlimited's Rhode Island-Maccan Project, just one of almost fifty valuable wetlands programs completed across Canada during 1969. The "duck's eye" view of the Rhode Island Project, located ten miles south of Amherst, Nova Scotia, clearly shows the Maccan River and portions of the 2,000 foot levee built by DU. The high-production, 210-acre marshland, boasting 2.6 miles of important shoreline, is sending Black Ducks and other waterfowl down our flyway this fall.
Courtesy Ducks Unlimited

ACKNOWLEDGEMENTS

ALLRED, WELLS — Agriculture and Waterfowl
BASSART, JACK — Photo Contributions
BAUER, EDDIE INC. — Les Kouba cover and paintings
BERNSEN, JOHN R. — Blind engineering
CAMERON, HOPE — Artist illustrations
CARLSON, BERT — Retrieving and Retrievers
COLLIER, RICHARD — Blind engineering
CROUSE, CARL — Director, Washington State Department of Game Duck
    and Goose distribution in Washington State
DIERDORFF, JACK — "Jack and the Cornstalk"
DOBBINS, JERRY — Blind engineering
DUCKS UNLIMITED — Photo contributions
DYE, HARRY — Duck Calling and Calls
ENG, JACK — Sweet & Sour Goose recipe and Sweet & Sour Sauce recipe
HERTER, GEORGE LEONARD — Photo contributions
HIRAI, PAUL & VIRGINIA — Orange Mallard recipe
JOHNSON, CHARLIE — "Duck Hunting — 1975"
JOHNSTON, JAMES W. — Legal
JONES, R. BRUCE — "Under Warranty?"
KOON, PHIL — "Dude Watching"
KOUBA, LES C. — Cover and goose paintings
McLEARY, EDWARD J. — Pilot, aerial location of blinds
PARK, JACK — Blueprint designs
SPRING, BOB & IRA — Photo contributions
U.S. FISH & WILDLIFE SERVICE — Biological, breeding, habitat and
    migration information of North American ducks and geese

We are grateful to the following manufacturers for their photo contributions:

BRANT DECOY
    L. L. Bean, Inc. Freeport, Maine 04032
BRUSH CUTTER
    Homelite Chain Saws, Port Chester, New York 10573
CLOTHING
    Eddie Bauer, Inc., Seattle, Washington 98134
    L. L. Bean, Inc., Freeport, Maine 04032
    Gokey Company, St. Paul, Minnesota 55102
    Herter's, Inc., Waseca, Minnesota 56093
COMMERCIAL BLINDS
    Smitty's Duck Blinds, Richmond, California 94804
DUCK CALLS
    Dye-Call Company, Seattle, Washington 98103
    Faulk's Game Call Company, Lake Charles, Louisiana 70601
    Herter's, Inc., Waseca, Minnesota 56093
    P. S. Olt Company, Pekin, Illinois 61554
DUCK DECOYS
    Dye-Call Company, Seattle, Washington 98103
    Eddie Bauer, Inc., Seattle, Washington 98134
    Herter's, Inc., Waseca, Minnesota 56093
    L. L. Bean, Inc., Freeport, Maine 04032
    Neumann & Bennetts, Inc., Klamath Falls, Oregon 97601
    Woodstream Corporation, Lititz, Pennsylvania 17543
DUCK FOODS
    Gunnersfield Enterprises, Maxwell, California 95955
GOOSE DECOYS
    Herter's, Inc., Waseca, Minnesota 56093
    William R. Johnson Co., Seattle, Washington 98101
    L. L. Bean, Inc., Freeport, Maine 04032
    Neumann & Bennetts, Inc., Klamath Falls, Oregon 97601
    Woodstream Corporation, Lititz, Pennsylvania 17543
GOOSE CALLS
    Faulks Game Call Company, Lake Charles, Louisiana 70601
    Herter's, Inc., Waseca, Minnesota 56093
    P. S. Olt Company, Pekin, Illinois 61554
GUNS
    Browning Arms Company, Morgan, Utah 84050
    The Garcia Corporation, Teaneck, New Jersey 07666
    Harrington & Richardson, Worcester, Massachusetts 01610
    Remington Arms Company, Bridgeport, Connecticut 06602
    Savage Arms, Westfield, Massachusetts 01085
    Winchester-Western, New Haven, Connecticut 06504
RETRIEVING AIDS
    Neumann & Bennetts, Inc., Klamath Falls, Oregon 97601
SHELLS
    Herter's, Inc., Waseca, Minnesota 56093

INDEX